Playing and Reality

'Winnicott was the greatest British psychoanalyst who ever lived. He writes beautifully and simply about the problems of everyday life – and is the perfect thing to read if you want to understand yourself and other people better.'

Alain de Botton

'He was a man who could be "popular" and completely accessible without ever ceasing to be profound, a man who ranged audaciously far and wide in the realms of thought but who always came back to home base, the psychology of the child.'

Oliver Sacks, The New York Times Book Review

Routledge Classics contains the very best of Routledge publishing over the past century or so, books that have, by popular consent, become established as classics in their field. Drawing on a fantastic heritage of innovative writing published by Routledge and its associated imprints, this series makes available in attractive, affordable form some of the most important works of modern times.

For a complete list of titles visit
www.routledgeclassics.com

D. W.
Winnicott

Playing and Reality

With a new preface by F. Robert Rodman,
North Carolina State University

 London and New York

First published 1971
by Tavistock Publications Ltd

First published in the USA in paperback in 1982

First published by Routledge in paperback in Great Britain in 1991

First published in Routledge Classics 2005
by Routledge
2 Park Square, Milton Park, Abingdon, Oxon, OX14 4RN

Simultaneously published in the USA and Canada
by Routledge
711 Third Avenue, New York, NY 10017 8th (Floor)

Routledge is an imprint of the Taylor & Francis Group, an informa business

© 1971 D. W. Winnicott
© 2005 Preface to the Routledge Classics edition, F. Robert Rodman

Typeset in Joanna by RefineCatch Limited, Bungay, Suffolk

British Library Cataloguing in Publication Data
A catalogue record for this book is available from the British Library

Library of Congress Cataloging in Publication Data
A catalog record for this book is available from the Library of Congress

ISBN10: 0–415–34546–4
ISBN13: 978–0–415–34546–0

To my patients
who have paid to teach me

10 Interrelating apart from Instinctual Drive and
    in terms of Cross-identifications   160
11 Contemporary Concepts of Adolescent
    Development and their Implications for
    Higher Education   186

TAILPIECE   204
REFERENCES   205
INDEX   209

Acknowledgements

I wish to thank Mrs Joyce Coles for her help in the preparation of the manuscript.

Also, I am much indebted to Masud Khan for his constructive criticisms of my writings and for his always being (as it seems to me) available when a practical suggestion is needed.

I have expressed my gratitude to my patients in my dedication.

For permission to reproduce material that has already appeared in print, thanks are due to the following: the Editor of *Child Psychology and Psychiatry*; the Editor of *Forum*; the Editor of the *International Journal of Psycho-Analysis*; the Editor of *Pediatrics*; the Editor of the International Library of Psycho-Analysis; Dr Peter Lomas; and the Hogarth Press Ltd, London.

PREFACE TO THE ROUTLEDGE CLASSICS EDITION

This collection of essays, prepared just before Winnicott's death in 1971, has been read and reread with profit by those interested in the ideas for their own sake, as well as all those who are trying to understand human beings in order to help them. In addition to a running description of his theory, Winnicott typically tells us over and over again what he means to get across. Each repetition adds some new element, as if in rehearsing these ideas he surprises himself with something new at the end of the trajectory of thought he has built up to that point. We, his readers, are the benefactors, because we get one chance after another to follow his development and to grasp the great arc of understanding that he brought to human development.

The paper on transitional objects (1953) starts the progression. It represents the summary achievement to that point of many preceding papers. The focus lies between baby and mother in the form of an object that is both created and discovered, which is the characteristic that yields freedom and joy to babies and all who were once babies. The mother provides what the baby is ready to imagine and in so doing she facilitates the baby's pleasure in a world that fosters its sense of omnipotence. The simple recognition of the meaning of soft toys and bits of blankets to babies, an understanding which, as Anna Freud put it, 'conquered the psychoanalytic world,' came into our grasp easily and obviously once Winnicott has explained it to us, although it had been overlooked by all until this point. Probably it took not only a child analyst but a pediatrician as well to perceive the significance of these materials. Winnicott started out and remained a pediatrician throughout his career. He estimated that in that time he had consulted with about 60,000 mother/child pairs.

He understood that the transition from having all its needs automatically met, in utero, to a capacity to accept the otherness of the external world, the child would have to develop over a long period of time during which the early sense of omnipotence was gradually succeeded by manageable frustrations. The same mother who provided the object that was made transitional is the mother that fails to meet the baby's needs according to its ability to grow as a result of the graduated failures.

With his theory of the transitional object, Winnicott jolted all ponderers on human nature into a realization of the neverending oscillation between the inner and the outer worlds. By implication, a state of dependency emerges as continuous in human life, and the environment therefore also as continuously important. Psychoanalysis, in the form of Freud's original and later theories, and Klein's especially had failed to appreciate this crucial fact. With Winnicott, we could take account of the role of the environment without at the same time losing the distinctly psychoanalytic awareness of the role of the inner life. And Winnicott's affirmation of Freud's work placed him in a continuous line of development in psychoanalysis, rather than play the role of a dissident. In spite of many opportunities to become the leader of the so-called object relations school, Winnicott declined, and turned away from any hint of discipleship among those who were influenced by him. He always believed that individual analysts had to find their own way, in effect to rediscover for themselves what others had found in their own way. This makes his work immensely appealing to younger therapists seeking a path that can make the most of their individual histories, talents and interests.

From transitional objects, through various papers on play and creativity, through considerations of culture as a development from transitional space, we get to the revolutionary ideas in his late paper on 'The Use of an Object.' Here Winnicott gives us a new awareness of personal factors in the creation of reality. He focuses on relationships that become 'of use.' Especially important individuals survive the continuous backdrop of unconscious destructive fantasy that inevitably accompanies closeness. That other person, by surviving the hate that emerges as a response to his or her otherness, attains a special status as a contributor to life, one who nourishes with what is genuinely new. This paper, coming near the end of Winnicott's life, opens pathways of thought for those who follow. Can it be true that all we perceive, the world out there, in the form of relationships as well as sensory perceptions, is observable insofar as it survives continuous fantasies of destruction? Can it be that we can tell that something is really 'out there' only if it continues to be there in spite of destructive processes emanating from ourselves? Recent work on the visual faculty seems to support the notion that the seen world is a constructed world, not a passively perceived one. Winnicott's theory, generated entirely from his own long study of human interaction, with its emphasis on a dynamic process of perception rooted in conflict, would seem to form a link between psychoanalysis and neurophysiology.

The arc of development of the ideas contained in this book gives us a compact, complex, and continuously enriching set of statements that are electrifying in their originality and the vastness of their implications. The book from its inception has remained in the forefront of psychoanalysis and remains as fresh today as it did when it first appeared.

No serious student of the mind can have overlooked *Playing and Reality*. As a result of the personal struggle that generated this array of contributions, Winnicott was able to liberate himself from the narrow orthodoxy imposed by Klein on the Freud she inherited, and to find his own path, based upon original observations and the struggle to make sense of them. Through his new language we come to grips with the primacy of play in all of life, the understanding of psychotherapy as the overlapping of the capacity to play in both patient and therapist, the value of cultural life as a derivative of transitional phenomena, and a host of other areas of interest. Experiences in the area of potential space allow us to have periods of rest from the struggle to draw lines between ourselves and others. There is a built-in strain in human life caused by the need to maintain a line that defines us as separate from others. This line need not confuse and exhaust the baby in possession of a transitional object, and a mother who understands his or her need for a particular kind of comfort. The resting place thus given continues to play the same role in the successive stages of human development. Playing makes it possible to address the otherness of reality. The world of playing, with its variations in the form of culture allows us to relax the barrier and refresh ourselves with shared experiences that do not require such delineations. Winnicott was famous for asking the question: What is there to live for? He brought this to the attention of therapists who may cure the ills of their patients but still not be able to answer his question. The compelling text of *Playing and Reality* is here to give us the answer.

F. ROBERT RODMAN, M.D.

INTRODUCTION

This book is a development of my paper 'Transitional Objects and Transitional Phenomena' (1951). First I wish to restate the basic hypothesis even though this involves repetition. Then I wish to introduce later developments that have taken place in my own thinking and in my assessment of clinical material. As I look back over the last decade I feel more and more impressed by the way in which this area of conceptualization has been neglected in the psychoanalytic conversation that is always taking place between analysts themselves and in the literature. This area of individual development and experience seems to have been neglected while attention was focused on psychic reality, which is personal and inner, and its relation to external or shared reality. Cultural experience has not found its true place in the theory used by analysts in their work and in their thinking.

It is, of course, possible to see that this which may be described as an intermediate area has found recognition in the work of philosophers. In theology it takes special shape in the eternal controversy over transubstantiation. It appears in full force in the work characteristic of the so-called metaphysical poets (Donne, etc.). My own approach derives from my study of babies and children, and in considering the place of these phenomena in the life of the child one must recognize the central position of Winnie the Pooh; I gladly add a reference to the Peanuts cartoons by Schulz. A phenomenon that is universal, like the one that I am considering in this book, cannot in fact be outside the range of those whose concern is the magic of imaginative and creative living.

It fell to my lot to be a psychoanalyst who, perhaps because of his having been a paediatrician, sensed the importance of this universal in the lives of infants and children, and wished to integrate his observation with the theory that we are all the time in the process of developing.

It is now generally recognized, I believe, that what I am referring to in this part of my work is not the cloth or the teddy bear that the baby uses – not so much the object used as the use of the object. I am drawing attention to the *paradox* involved in the use by the infant of what I have called the transitional object. My contribution is to ask for a paradox to be accepted and tolerated and respected, and for it not to be resolved. By flight to split-off intellectual functioning it is possible to resolve the paradox, but the price of this is the loss of the value of the paradox itself.

This paradox, once accepted and tolerated, has value for every human individual who is not only alive and living in this world but who is also capable of being infinitely enriched by exploitation of the cultural link with the past and with the future. It is this extension of the basic theme that concerns me in this book.

In writing this book around the subject of transitional phenomena. I find myself continuing to be reluctant to give examples. My reluctance belongs to the reason that I gave in the original paper; that examples can start to pin down specimens and begin a process of classification of an unnatural and arbitrary kind, whereas the thing that I am referring to is universal and has infinite variety. It is rather similar to the description of the human face when we describe one in terms of shape and eyes and nose and mouth and ears, but the fact remains that no two faces are exactly alike and very few are even similar. Two faces may be similar when at rest, but as soon as there is animation they become different. However, in spite of my reluctance I do not wish to neglect completely this kind of contribution.

Because these matters belong to the early stages of the development of every human being there is a wide-open clinical field awaiting exploration. An example would be the study by Olive Stevenson (1954), which was carried out when Miss Stevenson was a child care student at the London School of Economics. I am informed by Dr Bastiaans that it has become routine practice in Holland for medical students to include an inquiry into transitional objects and transitional phenomena when they are taking case-histories about children from their parents. The facts can teach.

Naturally, facts that can be elicited need to be interpreted, and for full use to be made of information given or observations made in a direct way on the behaviour of babies, these need to be placed in relation to a theory. In this way the same facts can seem to have one meaning for one observer and another meaning for another. Nevertheless, this is a promising field for direct observation and for indirect inquiry, and from time to time a student will be led by the results of his inquiries in this restricted field to recognize the complexity and the significance of the early stages of object-relating and of symbol-formation.

I know of one formal investigation into these matters and I wish to invite the reader to keep an open eye for publications coming from this quarter. Professor Renata Gaddini in Rome is making an elaborate study of transitional phenomena using three distinct social groupings, and she has already started to formulate ideas based on her observations. I find value in

Professor Gaddini's use of the idea of precursors, so that she is able to include in the whole subject the very early examples of fist-, finger-, and thumb-sucking and tongue-sucking, and all the complications that surround the use of a dummy or a pacifier. She also brings in the matter of rocking, both the child's rhythmical movement of the body and the rocking that belongs to cradles and human holding. Hair-pulling is an allied phenomenon.

Another attempt to work around the idea of the transitional object comes from Joseph C. Solomon of San Francisco, whose paper 'Fixed Idea as an Internalized Transitional Object' (1962) introduced a new concept. I am not sure how far I am in agreement with Dr Solomon, but the important thing is that with a theory of transitional phenomena at hand many old problems can be looked at afresh.

My own contribution here needs to be related to the fact that I am not now in a position to make the direct clinical observations of babies that have indeed been the main basis for everything I have built up into theory. I am still in touch, however, with descriptions that parents are able to give of their experiences with their children if we know how to give them the chance to remember in their own way and time. I am also in touch with children's own references to their own significant objects and techniques.

1

TRANSITIONAL OBJECTS AND TRANSITIONAL PHENOMENA

In this chapter I give the original hypothesis as formulated in 1951, and I then follow this up with two clinical examples.

I ORIGINAL HYPOTHESIS[1]

It is well known that infants as soon as they are born tend to use fist, fingers, thumbs in stimulation of the oral erotogenic zone, in satisfaction of the instincts at that zone, and also in quiet union. It is also well known that after a few months infants of either sex become fond of playing with dolls, and that most mothers allow their infants some special object and expect them to become, as it were, addicted to such objects.

---

[1] Published in the *International Journal of Psycho-Analysis*, Vol. 34, Part 2 (1953); and in D. W. Winnicott, *Collected Papers: Through Paediatrics to Psycho-Analysis* (1958a), London: Tavistock Publications.

There is a relationship between these two sets of phenomena that are separated by a time interval, and a study of the development from the earlier into the later can be profitable, and can make use of important clinical material that has been somewhat neglected.

The first possession

Those who happen to be in close touch with mothers' interests and problems will be already aware of the very rich patterns ordinarily displayed by babies in their use of the first 'not-me' possession. These patterns, being displayed, can be subjected to direct observation.

There is a wide variation to be found in a sequence of events that starts with the newborn infant's fist-in-mouth activities, and leads eventually on to an attachment to a teddy, a doll or soft toy, or to a hard toy.

It is clear that something is important here other than oral excitement and satisfaction, although this may be the basis of everything else. Many other important things can be studied, and they include:

1. The nature of the object.
2. The infant's capacity to recognize the object as 'not-me'.
3. The place of the object – outside, inside, at the border.
4. The infant's capacity to create, think up, devise, originate, produce an object.
5. The initiation of an affectionate type of object-relationship.

I have introduced the terms 'transitional objects' and 'transitional phenomena' for designation of the intermediate area of experience, between the thumb and the teddy bear, between the oral erotism and the true object-relationship, between primary creative activity and projection of what has already been introjected, between primary unawareness of indebtedness and the acknowledgement of indebtedness ('Say: "ta" ').

By this definition an infant's babbling and the way in which an older child goes over a repertory of songs and tunes while preparing for sleep come within the intermediate area as transitional phenomena, along with the use made of objects that are not part of the infant's body yet are not fully recognized as belonging to external reality.

Inadequacy of usual statement of human nature

It is generally acknowledged that a statement of human nature in terms of interpersonal relationships is not good enough even when the imaginative elaboration of function and the whole of fantasy both conscious and unconscious, including the repressed unconscious, are allowed for. There is another way of describing persons that comes out of the researches of the past two decades. Of every individual who has reached the stage of being a unit with a limiting membrane and an outside and an inside, it can be said that there is an *inner reality* to that individual, an inner world that can be rich or poor and can be at peace or in a state of war. This helps, but is it enough?

My claim is that if there is a need for this double statement, there is also need for a triple one: the third part of the life of a human being, a part that we cannot ignore, is an intermediate area of *experiencing*, to which inner reality and external life both contribute. It is an area that is not challenged, because no claim is made on its behalf except that it shall exist as a resting-place for the individual engaged in the perpetual human task of keeping inner and outer reality separate yet interrelated.

It is usual to refer to 'reality-testing', and to make a clear distinction between apperception and perception. I am here staking a claim for an intermediate state between a baby's inability and his growing ability to recognize and accept reality. I am therefore studying the substance of *illusion*, that which is allowed to the infant, and which in adult life is inherent in art and religion, and yet becomes the hallmark of madness when an adult puts too powerful a claim on the credulity of others, forcing them to acknowledge a sharing of illusion that is not their own. We can share a respect for *illusory experience*, and if we wish we may collect together and form a group on the basis of the similarity of our illusory experiences. This is a natural root of grouping among human beings.

I hope it will be understood that I am not referring exactly to the little child's teddy bear or to the infant's first use of the fist (thumb, fingers). I am not specifically studying the first object of object-relationships. I am concerned with the first possession, and with the intermediate area between the subjective and that which is objectively perceived.

Development of a personal pattern

There is plenty of reference in psychoanalytic literature to the progress from 'hand to mouth' to 'hand to genital', but perhaps less to further progress to the handling of truly 'not-me' objects. Sooner or later in an infant's development there comes a tendency on the part of the infant to weave other-than-me objects into the personal pattern. To some extent these objects stand for the breast, but it is not especially this point that is under discussion.

In the case of some infants the thumb is placed in the mouth while fingers are made to caress the face by pronation and supination movements of the forearm. The mouth is then active in relation to the thumb, but not in relation to the fingers. The fingers caressing the upper lip, or some other part, may be or may become more important than the thumb engaging the mouth. Moreover, this caressing activity may be found alone, without the more direct thumb-mouth union.

In common experience one of the following occurs, complicating an auto-erotic experience such as thumb-sucking:

(i)   with the other hand the baby takes an external object, say a part of a sheet or blanket, into the mouth along with the fingers; or
(ii)   somehow or other the bit of cloth is held and sucked, or not actually sucked; the objects used naturally include napkins and (later) handkerchiefs, and this depends on what is readily and reliably available; or
(iii)   the baby starts from early months to pluck wool and to collect it and to use it for the caressing part of the activity; less commonly, the wool is swallowed, even causing trouble; or
(iv)   mouthing occurs, accompanied by sounds of 'mum-mum', babbling, anal noises, the first musical notes, and so on.

One may suppose that thinking, or fantasying, gets linked up with these functional experiences.

All these things I am calling *transitional phenomena*. Also, out of all this (if we study any one infant) there may emerge some thing or some phenomenon perhaps a bundle of wool or the corner of a blanket or eiderdown, or a word or tune, or a mannerism – that becomes vitally important to the infant for use at the time of going to sleep, and is a defence against anxiety, especially anxiety of depressive type. Perhaps some soft object or other type of object has been found and used by the infant, and this then becomes what I am calling a *transitional object*. This object goes on being important. The parents get to know its value and carry it round when travelling. The mother lets it get dirty and even smelly, knowing that by washing it she introduces a break in continuity in the infant's experience, a break that may destroy the meaning and value of the object to the infant.

I suggest that the pattern of transitional phenomena begins to show at about four to six to eight to twelve months. Purposely I leave room for wide variations.

Patterns set in infancy may persist into childhood, so that the original soft object continues to be absolutely necessary at bedtime or at time of loneliness or when a depressed mood threatens. In health, however, there is a gradual extension of range of interest, and eventually the extended range is maintained, even when depressive anxiety is near. A need for a specific object or a behaviour pattern that started at a very early date may reappear at a later age when deprivation threatens.

This first possession is used in conjuction with special techniques derived from very early infancy, which can include or exist apart from the more direct auto-erotic activities. Gradually in the life of an infant teddies and dolls and hard toys are acquired. Boys to some extent tend to go over to use hard objects, whereas girls tend to proceed right ahead to the acquisition of a family. It is important to note, however, that there is no noticeable difference between boy and girl in their use of the original 'not-me' possession, which I am calling the transitional object.

As the infant starts to use organized sounds ('mum', 'ta', 'da') there may appear a 'word' for the transitional object. The name given by the infant to these earliest objects is often significant, and it usually has a word used by the adults partly incorporated in it. For instance, 'baa' may be the name, and the 'b' may have come from the adult's use of the word 'baby' or 'bear'.

I should mention that sometimes there is no transitional object except the mother herself. Or an infant may be so disturbed in emotional development that the transition state cannot be enjoyed, or the sequence of objects used is broken. The sequence may nevertheless be maintained in a hidden way.

Summary of special qualities in the relationship

1. The infant assumes rights over the object, and we agree to this assumption. Nevertheless, some abrogation of omnipotence is a feature from the start.

2. The object is affectionately cuddled as well as excitedly loved and mutilated.

3. It must never change, unless changed by the infant.

4. It must survive instinctual loving, and also hating and, if it be a feature, pure aggression.

5. Yet it must seem to the infant to give warmth, or to move, or to have texture, or to do something that seems to show it has vitality or reality of its own.

6. It comes from without from our point of view, but not so from the point of view of the baby. Neither does it come from within; it is not a hallucination.

7. Its fate is to be gradually allowed to be decathected, so that in the course of years it becomes not so much forgotten as rele gated to limbo. By this I mean that in health the transitional object does not 'go inside' nor does the feeling about it necessarily undergo repression. It is not forgotten and it is not mourned. It loses meaning, and this is because the transitional phenomena have become diffused, have become spread out over the whole intermediate territory between 'inner psychic reality' and 'the external world as perceived by two persons in common', that is to say, over the whole cultural field.

At this point my subject widens out into that of play, and of artistic creativity and appreciation, and of religious feeling, and of dreaming, and also of fetishism, lying and stealing, the origin and loss of affectionate feeling, drug addiction, the talisman of obsessional rituals, etc.

Relationship of the transitional object to symbolism

It is true that the piece of blanket (or whatever it is) is symbolical of some part-object, such as the breast. Nevertheless, the point of it is not its symbolic value so much as its actuality. Its not being the breast (or the mother), although real, is as important as the fact that it stands for the breast (or mother).

When symbolism is employed the infant is already clearly distinguishing between fantasy and fact, between inner objects and external objects, between primary creativity and perception. But the term transitional object, according to my suggestion, gives room for the process of becoming able to accept difference and similarity. I think there is use for a term for the root of symbolism in time, a term that describes the infant's journey from the purely subjective to objectivity; and it seems to me that the transitional object (piece of blanket, etc.) is what we see of this journey of progress towards experiencing.

It would be possible to understand the transitional object while not fully understanding the nature of symbolism. It seems that symbolism can be properly studied only in the process of the growth of an individual and that it has at the very best a variable meaning. For instance, if we consider the wafer of the Blessed Sacrament, which is symbolic of the body of Christ, I think I am right in saying that for the Roman Catholic community it is the body, and for the Protestant community it is a substitute, a reminder, and is essentially not, in fact, actually the body itself. Yet in both cases it is a symbol.

Clinical description of a transitional object

For anyone in touch with parents and children, there is an infinite quantity and variety of illustrative clinical material. The following illustrations are given merely to remind readers of similar material in their own experiences.

Two brothers: Contrast in early use of possessions

Distortion in use of transitional object. X, now a healthy man, has had to fight his way towards maturity. The mother 'learned how to be a mother' in her management of X when he was an infant and she was able to avoid certain mistakes with the other children because of what she learned with him. There were also external reasons why she was anxious at the time of her rather lonely management of X when he was born. She took her job as a mother very seriously and she breast-fed X for seven months. She feels that in his case this was too long and he was very difficult to wean. He never sucked his thumb or his fingers and when she weaned him 'he had nothing to fall back on'. He had never had the bottle or a dummy or any other form of feeding. He had a very strong and early *attachment to her herself*, as a person, and it was her actual person that he needed.

From twelve months he adopted a rabbit which he would cuddle, and his affectionate regard for the rabbit eventually transferred to real rabbits. This particular rabbit lasted till he was five or six years old. It could be described as a *comforter*, but it never had the true quality of a transitional object. It was never, as a true transitional object would have been, more important than the mother, an almost inseparable part of the infant. In the case of this particular boy the kinds of anxiety that were brought to a head by the weaning at seven months later produced asthma, and only gradually did he conquer this. It was important for him that he found employment far away from the home town. His attachment to his mother is still very powerful, although he comes within the wide definition of the term 'normal', or 'healthy'. This man has not married.

Typical use of transitional object. X's younger brother, Y, has developed in quite a straightforward way throughout. He now has three healthy children of his own. He was fed at the breast for four months and then weaned without difficulty. Y sucked his thumb in the early weeks and this again 'made weaning easier for him than for his older brother'. Soon after weaning at five to six months he adopted the end of the blanket where the stitching finished. He was pleased if a little bit of the wool stuck out at the corner and with this he would tickle his nose. This very early became his 'Baa'; he invented this word for it himself as soon as he could use organized sounds. From the time when he was about a year old he was able to substitute for the end of the blanket a soft green jersey with a red tie. This was not a 'comforter' as in the case of the depressive older brother, but a 'soother'. It was a sedative which always worked. This is a typical example of what I am calling a *transitional object*. When Y was a little boy it was always certain that if anyone gave him his 'Baa' he would immediately suck it and lose anxiety, and in fact he would go to sleep within a few minutes if the time for sleep were at all near. The thumb-sucking continued at the same time, lasting until he was three or four years old, and he remembers thumb-sucking and a hard place on one thumb which resulted from it. He is now interested (as a father) in the thumb-sucking of his children and their use of 'Baas'.

The story of seven ordinary children in this family brings out the following points, arranged for comparison in the table below.

Value in history-taking

In consultation with a parent it is often valuable to get information about the early techniques and possessions of all the children of the family. This starts the mother off on a comparison of her children one with another, and enables her to remember and compare their characteristics at an early age.

		Thumb	Transitional Object		Type of Child
X	Boy	o	Mother	Rabbit (comforter)	Mother-fixated
Y	Boy	+	'Baa'	Jersey (soother)	Free
Twins {	Girl	o	Dummy	Donkey (friend)	Late maturity
	Boy	o	'Ee'	Ee (protective)	Latent psychopathic
Children of Y {	Girl	o	'Baa'	Blanket (reassurance)	Developing well
	Girl	+	Thumb	Thumb (satisfaction)	Developing well
	Boy	+	'Mimis'	Objects (sorting)*	Developing well

* Added note: This was not clear, but I have left it as it was. D.W.W., 1971.

The child's contribution

Information can often be obtained from a child in regard to transitional objects. For instance:

> Angus (eleven years nine months) told me that his brother 'has tons of teddies and things' and 'before that he had little bears', and he followed this up with a talk about his own history. He said he never had teddies. There was a bell rope that hung down, a tag end of which he would go on hitting, and so go off to sleep. Probably in the end it fell, and that was the end of it. There was, however, something else. He was very shy about this. It was a purple rabbit with red eyes. 'I wasn't fond of it. I used to throw it around. Jeremy has it now, I gave it to him. I gave it to Jeremy because it was naughty. It *would* fall off the chest of drawers. *It still visits me. I like it to visit me.*' He surprised himself when he drew the purple rabbit.

It will be noted that this eleven-year-old boy with the ordinary good reality-sense of his age spoke as if lacking in reality-sense when describing the transitional object's qualities and activities. When I saw the mother later she expressed surprise that Angus remembered the purple rabbit. She easily recognized it from the coloured drawing.

Ready availability of examples

I deliberately refrain from giving more case-material here, particularly as I wish to avoid giving the impression that what I am reporting is rare. In practically every case-history there is something to be found that is interesting in the transitional phenomena, or in their absence.

Theoretical study

There are certain comments that can be made on the basis of accepted psychoanalytic theory:

1. The transitional object stands for the breast, or the object of the first relationship.
2. The transitional object antedates established reality-testing.
3. In relation to the transitional object the infant passes from (magical) omnipotent control to control by manipulation (involving muscle erotism and coordination pleasure).
4. The transitional object may eventually develop into a fetish object and so persist as a characteristic of the adult sexual life. (See Wulff's (1946) development of the theme.)
5. The transitional object may, because of anal erotic organization, stand for faeces (but it is not for this reason that it may become smelly and remain unwashed).

Relationship to internal object (Klein)

It is interesting to compare the transitional object concept with Melanie Klein's (1934) concept of the internal object. The transitional object is *not an internal object* (which is a mental concept) – it is a possession. Yet it is not (for the infant) an external object either.

The following complex statement has to be made. The infant can employ a transitional object when the internal object is alive and real and good enough (not too persecutory). But this internal object depends for its qualities on the existence and aliveness and behaviour of the external object. Failure of the latter in some essential function indirectly leads to deadness or to a persecutory quality of the internal object.[2] After a persistence of inadequacy of the external object the internal object fails to have meaning to the infant, and then, and then only, does the transitional object become meaningless too. The transitional object may therefore stand for the 'external' breast, but *indirectly*, through standing for an 'internal' breast.

The transitional object is never under magical control like the internal object, nor is it outside control as the real mother is.

Illusion-disillusionment

In order to prepare the ground for my own positive contribution to this subject I must put into words some of the things that I think are taken too easily for granted in many psychoanalytic writings on infantile emotional development, although they may be understood in practice.

There is no possibility whatever for an infant to proceed from the pleasure principle to the reality principle or towards and beyond primary identification (see Freud, 1923), unless there is a good-enough mother. The good-enough 'mother' (not necessarily the infant's own mother) is one who makes active adaptation to the infant's needs, an active adaptation that gradually lessens, according to the infant's growing ability to account for

[2] Text modified here, though based on the original statement.

failure of adaptation and to tolerate the results of frustration. Naturally, the infant's own mother is more likely to be good enough than some other person, since this active adaptation demands an easy and unresented preoccupation with the one infant; in fact, success in infant care depends on the fact of devotion, not on cleverness or intellectual enlightenment.

The good-enough mother, as I have stated, starts off with an almost complete adaptation to her infant's needs, and as time proceeds she adapts less and less completely, gradually, according to the infant's growing ability to deal with her failure.

The infant's means of dealing with this maternal failure include the following:

1. The infant's experience, often repeated, that there is a time-limit to frustration. At first, naturally, this time-limit must be short.
2. Growing sense of process.
3. The beginnings of mental activity.
4. Employment of auto-erotic satisfactions.
5. Remembering, reliving, fantasying, dreaming; the integrating of past, present, and future.

If all goes well the infant can actually come to gain from the experience of frustration, since incomplete adaptation to need makes objects real, that is to say hated as well as loved. The consequence of this is that if all goes well the infant can be disturbed by a close adaptation to need that is continued too long, not allowed its natural decrease, since exact adaptation resembles magic and the object that behaves perfectly becomes no better than a hallucination. Nevertheless, at the start adaptation needs to be almost exact, and unless this is so it is not possible for the infant to begin to develop a capacity to experience a relationship to external reality, or even to form a conception of external reality.

Illusion and the value of illusion

The mother, at the beginning, by an almost 100 per cent adaptation affords the infant the opportunity for the illusion that her breast is part of the infant. It is, as it were, under the baby's magical control. The same can be said in terms of infant care in general, in the quiet times between excitements. Omnipotence is nearly a fact of experience. The mother's eventual task is gradually to disillusion the infant, but she has no hope of success unless at first she has been able to give sufficient opportunity for illusion.

In another language, the breast is created by the infant over and over again out of the infant's capacity to love or (one can say) out of need. A subjective phenomenon develops in the baby, which we call the mother's breast.[3] The mother places the actual breast just there where the infant is ready to create, and at the right moment.

From birth, therefore, the human being is concerned with the problem of the relationship between what is objectively perceived and what is subjectively conceived of, and in the solution of this problem there is no health for the human being who has not been started off well enough by the mother. *The intermediate area to which I am referring is the area that is allowed to the infant between primary creativity and objective perception based on reality-testing.* The transitional phenomena represent the early stages of the use of illusion, without which there is no meaning for the human being in the idea of a relationship with an object that is perceived by others as external to that being.

The idea illustrated in Figure 1 is this: that at some theoretical point early in the development of every human individual an

---

[3] I include the whole technique of mothering. When it is said that the first object is the breast, the word 'breast' is used, I believe, to stand for the technique of mothering as well as for the actual flesh. It is not impossible for a mother to be a good-enough mother (in my way of putting it) with a bottle for the actual feeding.

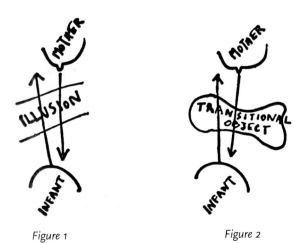

Figure 1   Figure 2

infant in a certain setting provided by the mother is capable of conceiving of the idea of something that would meet the growing need that arises out of instinctual tension. The infant cannot be said to know at first what is to be created. At this point in time the mother presents herself. In the ordinary way she gives her breast and her potential feeding urge. The mother's adaptation to the infant's needs, when good enough, gives the infant the illusion that there is an external reality that corresponds to the infant's own capacity to create. In other words, there is an overlap between what the mother supplies and what the child might conceive of. To the observer, the child perceives what the mother actually presents, but this is not the whole truth. The infant perceives the breast only in so far as a breast could be created just there and then. There is no interchange between the mother and the infant. Psychologically the infant takes from a breast that is part of the infant, and the mother gives milk to an infant that is part of herself. In psychology, the idea of interchange is based on an illusion in the psychologist.

In Figure 2 a shape is given to the area of illusion, to illustrate what I consider to be the main function of the transitional object and of transitional phenomena. The transitional object and the transitional phenomena start each human being off with what will always be important for them, i.e. a neutral area of experience which will not be challenged. *Of the transitional object it can be said that it is a matter of agreement between us and the baby that we will never ask the question: 'Did you conceive of this or was it presented to you from without?' The important point is that no decision on this point is expected. The question is not to be formulated.*

This problem, which undoubtedly concerns the human infant in a hidden way at the beginning, gradually becomes an obvious problem on account of the fact that the mother's main task (next to providing opportunity for illusion) is disillusionment. This is preliminary to the task of weaning, and it also continues as one of the tasks of parents and educators. In other words, this matter of illusion is one that belongs inherently to human beings and that no individual finally solves for himself or herself, although a theoretical understanding of it may provide a theoretical solution. If things go well, in this gradual disillusionment process, the stage is set for the frustrations that we gather together under the word 'weaning'; but it should be remembered that when we talk about the phenomena (which Klein (1940) has specifically illuminated in her concept of the depressive position) that cluster round weaning we are assuming the underlying process, the process by which opportunity for illusion and gradual disillusionment is provided. If illusion-disillusionment has gone astray the infant cannot get to so normal a thing as weaning, nor to a reaction to weaning, and it is then absurd to refer to weaning at all. The mere termination of breast-feeding is not a weaning.

We can see the tremendous significance of weaning in the case of the normal child. When we witness the complex reaction that is set going in a certain child by the weaning process, we know that this is able to take place in that child because the illusion-disillusionment process is being carried through so well that we can ignore it while discussing actual weaning.

Development of the theory of illusion-disillusionment

It is assumed here that the task of reality-acceptance is never completed, that no human being is free from the strain of relating inner and outer reality, and that relief from this strain is provided by an intermediate area of experience (cf. Riviere, 1936) which is not challenged (arts, religion, etc.). This intermediate area is in direct continuity with the play area of the small child who is 'lost' in play.

In infancy this intermediate area is necessary for the initiation of a relationship between the child and the world, and is made possible by good-enough mothering at the early critical phase. Essential to all this is continuity (in time) of the external emotional environment and of particular elements in the physical environment such as the transitional object or objects.

The transitional phenomena are allowable to the infant because of the parents' intuititive recognition of the strain inherent in objective perception, and we do not challenge the infant in regard to subjectivity or objectivity just here where there is the transitional object.

Should an adult make claims on us for our acceptance of the objectivity of his subjective phenomena we discern or diagnose madness. If, however, the adult can manage to enjoy the personal intermediate area without making claims, then we can acknowledge our own corresponding intermediate areas, and are pleased to find a degree of overlapping, that is to say common experience between members of a group in art or religion or philosophy.

Summary

Attention is drawn to the rich field for observation provided by the earliest experiences of the healthy infant as expressed principally in the relationship to the first possession.

This first possession is related backwards in time to auto-erotic phenomena and fist- and thumb-sucking, and also forwards to the first soft animal or doll and to hard toys. It is related both to the external object (mother's breast) and to internal objects (magically introjected breast), but is distinct from each.

Transitional objects and transitional phenomena belong to the realm of illusion which is at the basis of initiation of experience. This early stage in development is made possible by the mother's special capacity for making adaptation to the needs of her infant, thus allowing the infant the illusion that what the infant creates really exists.

This intermediate area of experience, unchallenged in respect of its belonging to inner or external (shared) reality, constitutes the greater part of the infant's experience, and throughout life is retained in the intense experiencing that belongs to the arts and to religion and to imaginative living, and to creative scientific work.

An infant's transitional object ordinarily becomes gradually decathected, especially as cultural interests develop.

What emerges from these considerations is the further idea that paradox accepted can have positive value. The resolution of paradox leads to a defence organization which in the adult one can encounter as true and false self organization (Winnicott, 1960a).

II AN APPLICATION OF THE THEORY

It is not the object, of course, that is transitional. The object represents the infant's transition from a state of being merged with the mother to a state of being in relation to the mother as something outside and separate. This is often referred to as the point at which the child grows up out of a narcissistic type of object-relating, but I have refrained from using this language because I am not sure that it is what I mean; also, it leaves out the idea of dependence, which is so essential at the earliest stages before the child has become sure that anything can exist that is not part of the child.

Psychopathology manifested in the area of transitional phenomena

I have laid great stress on the normality of transitional phenomena. Nevertheless, there is a psychopathology to be discerned in the course of the clinical examination of cases. As an example of the child's management of separation and loss I draw attention to the way in which separation can affect transitional phenomena.

As is well known, when the mother or some other person on whom the infant depends is absent, there is no immediate change owing to the fact that the infant has a memory or mental image of the mother, or what we call an internal representation of her, which remains alive for a certain length of time. If the mother is away over a period of time which is beyond a certain limit measured in minutes, hours, or days, then the memory or the internal representation fades. As this takes effect, the transitional phenomena become gradually meaningless and the infant is unable to experience them. We may watch the object becoming decathected. Just before loss we can sometimes see the exaggeration of the use of a transitional object as part of denial that there is a threat of its becoming meaningless. To illustrate this aspect of denial I shall give a short clinical example of a boy's use of string.

String[4]

A boy aged seven years was brought to the Psychology Department of the Paddington Green Children's Hospital by his mother and father in March 1955. The other two members of the family also came: a girl aged ten, attending an ESN school, and a rather normal small girl aged four. The case was referred by the family doctor because of a series of symptoms indicating a character disorder in the boy. An intelligence test gave the boy an IQ of 108. (For the purposes of this description all details that are not immediately relevant to the main theme of this chapter are omitted.)

I first saw the parents in a long interview in which they gave a clear picture of the boy's development and of the distortions in his development. They left out one important detail, however, which emerged in an interview with the boy.

It was not difficult to see that the mother was a depressive person, and she reported that she had been hospitalized on account of depression. From the parents' account I was able to note that the mother cared for the boy until the sister was born when he was three years three months. This was the first separation of importance, the next being at three years eleven months, when the mother had an operation. When the boy was four years nine months the mother went into a mental hospital for two months, and during this time he was well cared for by the mother's sister. By this time everyone looking after this boy agreed that he was difficult, although showing very good features. He was liable to change suddenly and to frighten people by saying, for instance, that he would cut his mother's sister into little pieces. He developed many curious symptoms, such as a

[4] Published in *Child Psychology and Psychiatry*, Vol. 1 (1960); and in Winnicott, *The Maturational Processes and the Facilitating Environment* (1965), London: Hogarth Press and the Institute of Psycho-Analysis.

compulsion to lick things and people; he made compulsive throat noises; often he refused to pass a motion and then made a mess. He was obviously anxious about his elder sister's mental defect, but the distortion of his development appears to have started before this factor became significant.

After this interview with the parents I saw the boy in a personal interview. There were present two psychiatric social workers and two visitors. The boy did not immediately give an abnormal impression and he quickly entered into a squiggle game with me. (In this squiggle game I make some kind of an impulsive line-drawing and invite the child whom I am interviewing to turn it into something, and then he makes a squiggle for me to turn into something in my turn.)

The squiggle game in this particular case led to a curious result. The boy's laziness immediately became evident, and also nearly everything I did was translated by him into something associated with string. Among his ten drawings there appeared the following:

lasso
whip
crop
a yo-yo string
a string in a knot
another crop
another whip.

After this interview with the boy I had a second one with the parents, and asked them about the boy's preoccupation with string. They said that they were glad that I had brought up this subject, but they had not mentioned it because they were not sure of its significance. They said that the boy had become obsessed with everything to do with string, and in fact whenever they went into a room they were liable to find that he had joined together chairs and tables; and they might find a cushion, for instance, with a string joining it to the fireplace. They said that the boy's preoccupation with string was gradually developing a new feature, one that had worried them instead of causing them ordinary concern. He had recently tied a string round his sister's neck (the sister whose birth provided the first separation of this boy from his mother).

In this particular kind of interview I knew I had limited opportunity for action: it would not be possible to see these parents or the boy more frequently than once in six months, since the family lived in the country. I therefore took action in the following way. I explained to the mother that this boy was dealing with a fear of separation, attempting to deny separation by his use of string, as one would deny separation from a friend by using the telephone. She was sceptical, but I told her that should she come round to finding some sense in what I was saying I should like her to open up the matter with the boy at some convenient time, letting him know what I had said, and then developing the theme of separation according to the boy's response.

I heard no more from these people until they came to see me about six months later. The mother did not report to me what she had done, but I asked her and she was able to tell me what had taken place soon after the visit to me. She had felt that what I had said was silly, but one evening she had opened the subject with the boy and found him to be eager to talk about his relation to her and his fear of a lack of contact with her. She went over all the separations she could think of with him with his help, and she soon became convinced that what I had said was right, because of his responses. Moreover, from the moment that she had this conversation with him the string play ceased. There was no more joining of objects in the old way. She had had many other conversations with the boy about his feeling of separateness from her, and she made the very significant comment that she felt the most important separation to have been his loss of her when she was seriously depressed; it was not just her going away, she said, but her lack of contact with him because of her complete preoccupation with other matters.

At a later interview the mother told me that a year after she had had her first talk with the boy there was a return to playing with string and to joining together objects in the house. She was in fact due to go into hospital for an operation, and she said to him: 'I can see from your playing with string that you are worried about my going away, but this time I shall only be away a few days, and I am having an operation which is not serious.' After this conversation the new phase of playing with string ceased.

I have kept in touch with this family and have helped with various details in the boy's schooling and other matters. Recently, four years after the original interview, the father reported a new phase of string preoccupation, associated with a fresh depression in the mother. This phase lasted two months; it cleared up when the whole family went on holiday, and when at the same time there was an improvement in the home situation (the father having found work after a period of unemployment). Associated with this was an improvement in the mother's state. The father gave one further interesting detail relevant to the subject under discussion. During this recent phase the boy had acted out something with rope which the father felt to be significant, because it showed how intimately all these things were connected with the mother's morbid anxiety. He came home one day and found the boy hanging upside down on a rope. He was quite limp and acting very well as if dead. The father realized that he must take no notice, and he hung around the garden doing odd jobs for half an hour, after which the boy got bored and stopped the game. This was a big test of the father's lack of anxiety. On the following day, however, the boy did the same thing from a tree which could easily be seen from the kitchen window. The mother rushed out severely shocked and certain that he had hanged himself.

The following additional detail might be of value in the understanding of the case. Although this boy, who is now eleven, is developing along 'tough-guy' lines, he is very self-conscious and easily goes red in the neck. He has a number of teddy bears which to him are children. No one dares to say that they are toys. He is loyal to them, expends a great deal of affection over them, and makes trousers for them, which involves careful sewing. His father says that he seems to get a sense of security from his family, which he mothers in this way. If visitors come he quickly puts them all into his sister's bed, because no one outside the family must know that he has this family. Along with this is a reluctance to defaecate, or a tendency to save up his faeces. It is not difficult to guess, therefore, that he has a maternal identification based on his own insecurity in relation to his mother, and that this could develop into homosexuality. In the same way the preoccupation with string could develop into a perversion.

Comment

The following comment seems to be appropriate.

1. String can be looked upon as an extension of all other techniques of communication. String joins, just as it also helps in the wrapping up of objects and in the holding of unintegrated material. In this respect string has a symbolic meaning for everyone; an exaggeration of the use of string can easily belong to the beginnings of a sense of insecurity or the idea of a lack of communication. In this particular case it is possible to detect abnormality creeping into the boy's use of string, and it is important to find a way of stating the change which might lead to its use becoming perverted.

It would seem possible to arrive at such a statement if one takes into consideration the fact that the function of the string is changing from communication into a *denial of separation*. As a denial of separation string becomes a thing in itself, something that has dangerous properties and must needs be mastered. In this case the mother seems to have been able to deal with the boy's use of string just before it was too late, when the use of it still contained hope. When hope is absent and string represents a denial of separation, then a much more complex state of affairs has arisen – one that becomes difficult to cure, because of the secondary gains that arise out of the skill that develops whenever an object has to be handled in order to be mastered.

This case therefore is of special interest if it makes possible the observation of the development of a perversion.

2. It is also possible to see from this material the use that can be made of parents. When parents can be used they can work with great economy, especially if the fact is kept in mind that there will never be enough psychotherapists to treat all those who are in need of treatment. Here was a good family that had been through a difficult time because of the father's unemployment; that had been able to take full responsibility for a backward girl in spite of the tremendous drawbacks, socially and within the family, that this entails; and that had survived the bad phases in the mother's depressive illness, including one phase of hospitalization. There must be a great deal of strength in such a family, and it was on the basis of this assumption that the decision was made to invite these parents to undertake the therapy of their own child. In doing this they learned a great deal themselves, but they did need to be informed about what they were doing. They also needed their success to be appreciated and the whole process to be verbalized. The fact that they have seen their boy through an illness has given the parents confidence with regard to their ability to manage other difficulties that arise from time to time.

Added note 1969

In the decade since this report was written I have come to see that this boy could not be cured of his illness. The tie-up with the mother's depressive illness remained, so that he could not be kept from running back to his home. Away, he could have had personal treatment, but at home personal treatment was impracticable. At home he retained the pattern that was already set at the time of the first interview.

In adolescence this boy developed new addictions, especially to drugs, and he could not leave home in order to receive education. All attempts to get him placed away from his mother failed because he regularly escaped and ran back home.

He became an unsatisfactory adolescent, lying around and apparently wasting his time and his intellectual potential (as noted above, he had an IQ of 108).

The question is: would an investigator making a study of this case of drug addiction pay proper respect to the psycho-pathology manifested in the area of transitional phenomena?

III CLINICAL MATERIAL: ASPECTS OF FANTAS

In the later part of this book I shall explore some of the ideas that occur to me while I am engaged in clinical work and where I feel that the theory I have formed for my own benefit in regard to transitional phenomena affects what I see and hear and what I do.

Here I shall give in detail some clinical material from an adult patient to show how the sense of loss itself can become a way of integrating one's self-experience.

The material is of one session of a woman patient's analysis, and I give it because it collects together various examples of the great variety that characterizes the vast area between objectivity and subjectivity.

This patient, who has several children, and who has a high intelligence which she uses in her work, comes to treatment because of a wide range of symptomatology which is usually collected together under the word 'schizoid'. It is probable that those who have dealings with her do not recognize how ill she feels, and certainly she is usually liked and is felt to have value.

This particular session started with a dream which could be described as depressive. It contained straightforward and revealing transference material with the analyst as an avaricious dominating woman. This leaves way for her hankering after a former analyst who is very much a male figure for her. This is dream, and as dream could be used as material for interpretation. The patient was pleased that she was dreaming more. Along with this she was able to describe certain enrichments in her actual living in the world.

Every now and again she is overtaken by what might be called *fantasying*. She is going on a train journey; there is an accident. How will the children know what has happened to her? How indeed will her analyst know? She might be screaming, but her mother would not hear. From this she went on to talk about her most awful experience in which she left a cat for a little while and she heard afterwards that the cat had been crying for several hours. This is 'altogether too awful' and joins up with the very many separations she experienced throughout her childhood, separations that went beyond her capacity to allow for, and were therefore traumatic, necessitating the organization of new sets of defences.

Much of the material in this analysis has to do with coming to the negative side of relationships; that is to say, with the gradual failure that has to be experienced by the child when the parents are not available. The patient is extremely sensitive to all this in regard to her own children and ascribes much of the difficulty that she has with her first child to the fact that she left this child for three days to go for a holiday with her husband when she had started a new pregnancy; that is to say, when the child was nearly two. She was told that the child had cried for four hours without stopping, and when she came home it was no use for quite a long time for her to try to re-establish rapport.

We were dealing with the fact that animals and small children cannot be told what is happening. The cat could not understand. Also, a baby under two years cannot be properly informed about a new baby that is expected, although 'by twenty months or so' it becomes increasingly possible to explain this in words that a baby can understand.

When no understanding can be given, then when the mother is away to have a new baby she is dead from the point of view of the child. This is what dead means.

It is a matter of days or hours or minutes. Before the limit is reached the mother is still alive; after this limit has been overstepped she is dead. In between is a precious moment of anger, but this is quickly lost, or perhaps never experienced, always potential and carrying fear of violence.

From here we come to the two extremes, so different from each other: the death of the mother when she is present, and her death when she is not able to reappear and therefore to come alive again. This has to do with the time just before the child has built up the ability to bring people alive in the inner psychic reality apart from the reassurance of seeing, feeling, smelling.

It can be said that this patient's childhood had been one big exercise exactly in this area. She was evacuated because of the war when she was about eleven; she completely forgot her childhood and her parents, but all the time she steadily maintained the right not to call those who were caring for her 'uncle' and 'auntie', which was the usual technique. She managed *never to call them anything* the whole of those years, and this was the negative of remembering her mother and father. It will be understood that the pattern for all this was set up in her early childhood.

From this my patient reached the position, which again comes into the transference, that the only real thing is the gap; that is to say, the death or the absence or the amnesia. In the course of the session she had a specific amnesia and this bothered her, and it turned out that the important communication for me to get was that there could be a blotting out, and that this blank could be the only fact and the only thing that was real. The amnesia is real, whereas what is forgotten has lost its reality.

In connection with this the patient remembered that there is a rug available in the consulting-room which she once put around herself and once used for a regressive episode during an analytic session. At present she is not going over to fetch this rug or using it. The reason is that the rug that is not there (because she does not go for it) is more real than the rug that the analyst might bring, as he certainly had the idea to do. Consideration of this brings her up against the absence of the rug, or perhaps it would be better to say against the unreality of the rug in its symbolic meaning.

From here there was a development in terms of the idea of symbols. The last of her former analysts 'will always be more important to me than my present analyst'. She added: 'You may do me more good, but I like him better. This will be true when I have completely forgotten him. The negative of him is more real than the positive of you.' These may not be exactly her words but it is what she was conveying to me in clear language of her own, and it was what she needed me to understand.

The subject of nostalgia comes into the picture: it belongs to the precarious hold that a person may have on the inner representation of a lost object. This subject reappears in the case-report that follows (see p. 49).

The patient then talked about her imagination and the limits of what she believed to be real. She started by saying: 'I didn't really believe that there was an angel standing by my bed; on the other hand, I used to have an eagle chained to my wrist.' This certainly did feel real to her and the accent was on the words 'chained to my wrist.' She also had a white horse which was as real as possible and she 'would ride it everywhere and hitch it to a tree and all that sort of thing'. She would like really to own a white horse now so as to be able to deal with the reality of this white horse experience and make it real in another way. As she spoke I felt how easily these ideas could be labelled hallucinatory except in the context of her age at the time and her exceptional experiences in regard to repeated loss of otherwise good parents. She exclaimed: 'I suppose I want something that never goes away.' We formulated this by saying that the real thing is the thing that is not there. The chain is a denial of the eagle's absence, which is the positive element.

From here we got on to the symbols that fade. She claimed that she had had some success in making her symbols real for a long time in spite of the separations. We both came to something here at the same time, which is that her very fine intellect has been exploited, but at cost. She read from very early, and read a great deal; she has done a great deal of thinking from the earliest times and she has always used her intellect to keep things going and she has enjoyed this; but she was relieved (I thought) when I told her that with this use of the intellect there is all the time a fear of mental defect. From this she quickly reached over to her interest in autistic children and her intimate tie-up with a friend's schizophrenia, a condition that illustrates the idea of mental defect in spite of good intellect. She has felt tremendously guilty about having a great pride in her good intellect, which has always been a rather obvious feature. It was difficult for her to think that perhaps her friend may have had a good intellectual potential although in his case it would be necessary to say that he had slipped over into the obverse, which is mental retardation through mental illness.

She described various techniques for dealing with separation; for instance: a paper spider and pulling the legs off for every day that her mother was away. Then she also had flashes, as she called them, and she would suddenly see, for instance, her dog Toby, a toy: 'Oh there's Toby.' There is a picture in the family album of herself with Toby, a toy, that she has forgotten except in the flashes. This led on to a terrible incident in which her mother had said to her: 'But we "heard" you cry all the time we were away.' They were four miles apart. She was two years old at the time and she thought: 'Could it possibly be that my mother told me a lie?' She was not able to cope with this at the time and she tried to deny what she really knew to be true, that her mother had in fact lied. It was difficult to believe in her mother in this guise because everyone said: 'Your mother is so marvellous.'

From this it seemed possible for us to reach to an idea which was rather new from my point of view. Here was the picture of a child and the child had transitional objects, and there were transitional phenomena that were evident, and all of these were symbolical of something and were real for the child; but gradually, or perhaps frequently for a little while, she had to *doubt the reality of the thing that they were symbolizing*. That is to say, if they were symbolical of her mother's devotion and reliability they remained real in themselves but what they stood for was not real. The mother's devotion and reliability were unreal.

This seemed to be near the sort of thing that has haunted her all her life, losing animals, losing her own children, so that she formulated the sentence: 'All I have got is what I have not got.' There is a desperate attempt here to turn the negative into a last-ditch defence against the end of everything. The negative is the only positive. When she got to this point she said to her analyst: 'And what will you do about it?' I was silent and she said: 'Oh, I see.' I thought perhaps that she was resenting my masterly inactivity. I said: 'I am silent because I don't know what to say.' She quickly said that this was all right. Really she was glad about the silence, and she would have preferred it if I had said nothing at all. Perhaps as a silent analyst I might have been joined up with the former analyst that she knows she will always be looking for. She will always expect him to come back and say 'Well done!' or something. This will be long after she has forgotten what he looks like. I was thinking that her meaning was: when he has become sunk in the general pool of subjectivity and joined up with what she thought she found when she had a mother and before she began to notice her mother's deficiencies as a mother, that is to say, her absences.

Conclusion

In this session we had roamed over the whole field between subjectivity and objectivity, and we ended up with a bit of a game. She was going on a railway journey to her holiday house and she said: 'Well I think you had better come with me, perhaps half-way.' She was talking about the way in which it matters to her very much indeed that she is leaving me. This was only for a week, but there was a rehearsal here for the summer holiday. It was also saying that after a little while, when she has got away from me, it will not matter any longer. So, at a half-way station, I get out and 'come back in the hot train', and she derided my maternal identification aspects by adding: 'And it will be very tiring, and there will be a lot of children and babies, and they will climb all over you, and they will probably be sick all over you, and serve you right.'

(It will be understood that there was no idea of my *really* accompanying her.)

Just before she went she said. 'Do you know I believe when I went away at the time of evacuation [in the war] I could say that *I went to see if my parents were there*. I seem to have believed I would find them there.' (This implied that they were certainly not to be found at home.) And the implication was that she took a year or two to find the answer. The answer was that they were not there, and that *that* was reality. She had already said to me about the rug that she did not use: 'You know, don't you, that the rug might be very comfortable, but reality is more important than comfort and *no rug* can therefore be more important than *a rug*.'

This clinical fragment illustrates the value of keeping in mind the distinctions that exist between phenomena in terms of their position in the area between external or shared reality and the true dream.

2

DREAMING, FANTASYING AND LIVING

A case-history describing a Primary Dissociation

In this chapter I make a fresh attempt to show the subtle qualitative differences that exist between varieties of fantasying. I am looking particularly at what has been called fantasying and I use once more the material of a session in a treatment where the contrast between fantasying and dreaming was not only relevant but, I would say, central.[1]

The case I am using is that of a woman of middle age who in her analysis is gradually discovering the extent to which fantasying or something of the nature of daydreaming has

---

[1] For discussion of this theme from another angle see 'The Manic Defence' (1935) in Winnicott (1958a).

disturbed her whole life. What has now become clear is that there is an essential difference for her between fantasying and the alternatives of dreaming, on the one hand, and of real living and relating to real objects, on the other. With unexpected clarity, dreaming and living have been seen to be of the same order, daydreaming being of another order. Dream fits into object-relating in the real world, and living in the real world fits into the dream-world in ways that are quite familiar, especially to psychoanalysts. By contrast, however, fantasying remains an isolated phenomenon, absorbing energy but not contributing-in either to dreaming or to living. To some extent fantasying has remained static over the whole of this patient's life, that is to say, dating from very early years, the pattern being established by the time that she was two or three. It was in evidence at an even earlier date, and it probably started with a 'cure' of thumb-sucking.

Another distinguishing feature between these two sets of phenomena is this, that whereas a great deal of dream and of feelings belonging to life are liable to be under repression, this is a different kind of thing from the inaccessibility of the fantasying. Inaccessibility of fantasying is associated with dissociation rather than with repression. Gradually, as this patient begins to become a whole person and begins to lose her rigidly organized dissociations, so she becomes aware[2] of the vital importance that fantasying has always had for her. At the same time the fantasying is changing into imagination related to dream and reality.

The qualitative differences can be extremely subtle and difficult to describe; nevertheless the big differences belong to the presence or the absence of a dissociated state. For instance, the patient is in my room having her treatment and a little bit of the sky is available for her to look at. It is evening. She says: 'I am up on those pink clouds where I can walk.' This, of course, might be an imaginative flight. It could be part of the way in

---

[2] She has a place from which to become aware.

which the imagination enriches life just as it could be material for dream. At the same time, for my patient this very thing can be something that belongs to a dissociated state, and it may not become conscious in the sense that there is never a whole person there to be aware of the two or more dissociated states that are present at any one time. The patient may sit in her room and while doing nothing at all except breathe she has (in her fantasy) painted a picture, or she has done an interesting piece of work in her job, or she has been for a country walk; but from the observer's point of view nothing whatever has happened. In fact, nothing is likely to happen because of the fact that in the dissociated state so much is happening. On the other hand, she may be sitting in her room thinking of tomorrow's job and making plans, or thinking about her holiday, and this may be an imaginative exploration of the world and of the place where dream and life are the same thing. In this way she swings from well to ill, and back again to well.

It will be observed that a time factor is operative which is different according to whether she is fantasying or imagining. In the fantasying, what happens happens immediately, except that it does not happen at all. These similar states are recognized as different in the analysis because of the fact that if the analyst looks for them he always has indications of the degree of dissociation that is present. Often the difference between the two examples cannot be discerned from a verbal description of what goes on in the patient's mind, and would be lost in a tape-recording of the work of the session.

This particular woman has rather exceptional talents or potential for various kinds of artistic self-expression and she knows enough about life and living and about her potential to realize that in life terms she is missing the boat, and that she has always been missing the boat (at least, from near the beginning of her life). Inevitably she is a disappointment to herself and to all those relations and friends who feel hopeful about her. She feels when people are hopeful about her that they are expecting something of her or from her, and this brings her up against her essential inadequacy. All this is a matter for intense grief and resentment in the patient and there is plenty of evidence that without help she was in danger of suicide, which would simply have been the nearest that she could get to murder. If she gets near to murder she begins to protect her object so at that point she has the impulse to kill herself and in this way to end her difficulties by bringing about her own death and the cessation of the difficulties. Suicide brings no solution, only cessation of struggle.

There is an extremely complex aetiology in any case like this, but it is possible to say something brief about this patient's early childhood in a language which has some validity. It is true that a pattern was established in her early relationship to her mother, a relationship that too abruptly and too early became changed from very satisfactory to disillusionment and despair and the abandonment of hope in object-relating. There could also be a language for describing this same pattern in the little girl's relationship to her father. The father to some extent corrected where the mother had failed, and yet in the end he got caught up in the pattern that was becoming part of the child, so that he also failed essentially, especially as he thought of her as a potential woman and ignored the fact that she was potentially male.[3]

The simplest way to describe the beginnings of this pattern in this patient is to think of her as a little girl with several older siblings, she being the youngest. These children were left to look after themselves a good deal, partly because they seemed to be able to enjoy themselves and to organize their own games and their own management with ever-increasing enrichment. This youngest child, however, found herself in a world that was already organized before she came into the nursery. She was very

---

[3] For a discussion of male and female elements, see Chapter 5.

intelligent and she managed somehow or other to fit in. But she was never really very rewarding as a member of the group from her own or from the other children's point of view, because she could fit in only on a compliance basis. The games were unsatisfactory for her because she was simply struggling to play whatever role was assigned to her, and the others felt that something was lacking in the sense that she was not actively contributing-in. It is likely, however, that the older children were not aware that their sister was essentially absent. From the point of view of my patient, as we now discover, while she was playing the other people's games she was *all the time engaged in fantasying*. She really lived in this fantasying on the basis of a dissociated mental activity. This part of her which became thoroughly dissociated was never the whole of her, and over long periods her defence was to live here in this fantasying activity, and to watch herself playing the other children's games as if watching someone else in the nursery group.

By means of the dissociation, reinforced by a series of significant frustrations in which her attempts to be a whole person in her own right met with no success, she became a specialist in this one thing: being able to have a dissociated life while seeming to be playing with the other children in the nursery. The dissociation was never complete and the statement that I have made about the relationship between this child and the siblings was probably never entirely applicable, but there is enough truth in this kind of statement to enable a description to be usefully made in these terms.

As my patient grew older so she managed to construct a life in which nothing that was really happening was fully significant to her. Gradually she became one of the many who do not feel that they exist in their own right as whole human beings. All the time, without her knowing it, while she was at school and later at work, there was another life going on in terms of the part that was dissociated. Put the other way around, this meant that her life was dissociated from the main part of her, which was living in what became an organized sequence of fantasying.

If one were to trace this patient's life one could see the ways in which she attempted to bring together these two and other parts of her personality, but her attempts always had some kind of protest in them which brought a clash with society. All the time she had enough health to continue to give promise and to make her relations and her friends feel that she would make her mark, or at any rate that she would one day enjoy herself. To fulfil this promise was impossible, however, because (as she and I have gradually and painfully discovered) the main part of her existence was taking place when she was doing nothing whatever. Doing nothing whatever was perhaps disguised by certain activities which she and I came to refer to as thumb-sucking. Later versions of this took the form of compulsive smoking and various boring and obsessive games. These and other futile activities brought no joy. All they did was to fill the gap, and this gap was an essential state of doing nothing while she was doing everything. She became frightened during the analysis because she could see that this could very easily have led to her lying all her life in a bed in a mental hospital, incontinent, inactive and immobile, and yet in her mind keeping up a continuity of fantasying in which omnipotence was retained and wonderful things could be achieved in a dissociated state.[4]

As soon as this patient began to put something into practice, such as to paint or to read, she found the limitations that made her dissatisfied because she had let go of the omnipotence that she retained in the fantasying. This could be referred to in terms

[4] This is quite different from that 'experience of omnipotence' which I have described as an essential process in the first experiences of the 'me' and the 'not-me' (cf. Winnicott, 1962; see also p. 47 below). The 'experience of omnipotence' belongs essentially to dependence, whereas this omnipotence belongs to hopelessness about dependence.

of the reality principle but it is more true, in the case of a patient like this, to speak of the dissociation that was a fact in her personality structure. In so far as she was healthy and in so far as at certain times she acted like a whole person she was quite capable of dealing with the frustrations that belong to the reality principle. In the ill state, however, no capacity for this was needed because reality was not encountered.

Perhaps this patient's state could be illustrated by two of her dreams.

Two dreams

1. She was in a room with many people and she knew that she was engaged to be married to a slob. She described a man of a kind that she would not in fact like. She turned to her neighbour and said: 'That man is the father of my child.' In this way, with my help, she informed herself at this late stage in her analysis that she has a child, and she was able to say that the child was about ten years old. In point of fact she has no child, yet she could see from this dream that she has had a child for many years and that the child is growing up. Incidentally this accounted for one of the early remarks she made in the session, which was to ask: 'Tell me, do I dress too much like a child, considering that I am middle-aged?' In other words, she was very near to recognizing that she has to dress for this child as well as for her middle-aged self. She could tell me that the child was a girl.

2. There was a previous dream in a session a week earlier in which she felt intense resentment against her mother (to whom she is potentially devoted) because, as it came in the dream, her mother had deprived her daughter, that is herself, of her own children. She felt it was queer that she had dreamed in this way. She said: 'The funny thing is that here I look as if I am wanting a child, whereas in my conscious thought I know that I only think of children as needing protection from being born.' She added:

'It is as if I have a sneaking feeling that some people do find life not too bad.'

Naturally, as in every case, there is a great deal else that could be reported around these dreams which I omit because it would not necessarily throw light on the exact problem that I am examining.

The patient's dream about that man being the father of her child was given without any sense of conviction and without any link with feeling. It was only after the session had lasted an hour and a half that the patient began to reach to feeling. Before she went, at the end of two hours, she had experienced a wave of hate of her mother which had a new quality to it. It was much nearer to murder than to hate and also it felt to her that the hate was much nearer than it had previously been to a specific thing. She could now think that the slob, the father of her child, was put forward as a slob to disguise from her mother that it was her father, her mother's husband, who was the father of her child. This meant that she was very close to the feeling of being murdered by her mother. Here we were indeed dealing with dream and with life, and we were not lost in fantasying.

These two dreams are given to show how material that had formerly been locked in the fixity of fantasying was now becoming released for both dreaming and living, two phenomena that are in many respects the same. In this way the difference between daydreaming and dreaming (which is living) was gradually becoming clearer to the patient, and the patient was gradually becoming able to make the distinction clear to the analyst. It will be observed that creative playing is allied to dreaming and to living but essentially does not belong to fantasying. Thus significant differences begin to appear in the theory of the two sets of phenomena although it remains difficult to make a pronouncement or a diagnosis when an example is given.

The patient posed the question: 'When I am walking up on that pink cloud, is that my imagination enriching life or is it this thing that you are calling fantasying which happens when I am doing nothing and which makes me feel that I do not exist?'

For me the work of this session had produced an important result. It had taught me that fantasying interferes with action and with life in the real or external world, but much more so it interferes with dream and with the personal or inner psychic reality, the living core of the individual personality.

It could be valuable to look at the subsequent two sessions in this patient's analysis.

The patient started with: 'You were talking about the way in which fantasying interferes with dreaming. That night I woke at midnight and there I was hectically cutting out, planning, working on the pattern for a dress. I was all but doing it and was het-up. Is that dreaming or fantasying? I became aware of what it was all about but I was awake.'

I found this question difficult because it seemed to be on the borderline in any attempt one might make to differentiate between fantasying and dreaming. There was psychosomatic involvement. I said to the patient: 'We don't know, do we!' I said this simply because it was true.

We talked around the subject, how the fantasying is unconstructive and damaging to the patient and makes her feel ill. Certainly working herself up in this way restricts her from action. She talked about the way in which she often uses radio to hear talks rather than music, while playing patience. This experience seems to play into the dissociation almost as if it is making use of it and therefore giving her some degree of a sense that there might be an integration or a breakdown of the dissociation. I pointed this out to her and she gave me an example at the moment while I was talking. She said that while I was talking she was fiddling with the zip of her bag: why was it this end? how awkward it was to do up! She could feel that this dissociated activity was more important to her sitting there than listening to what I was saying. We both tried to make an attack on the subject in hand and to relate fantasying to dreaming. Suddenly she had a little insight and said that the meaning of this fantasying was: 'So that's what *you* think.' She had taken my interpretation of the dream and she had tried to make it foolish. There was evidently a dream which turned into this fantasying as she woke, and she wanted to make it quite clear to me that she was awake while fantasying. She said: 'We need another word, which is neither dream nor fantasy.' At this moment she reported that she had already 'gone off to her job and to things that happened at work' and so here again while talking to me she had left me, and she felt dissociated as if she could not be in her skin. She remembered how she read the words of a poem but the words meant nothing. She made the remark that this kind of involvement of her body in the fantasying produces great tension, but since nothing is happening this makes her feel that she is a candidate for a coronary occlusion or for high blood pressure, or for gastric ulcers (which indeed she has had). How she longs to find something that will make her do things, to use every waking minute, to be able to say: 'It is now and not tomorrow, tomorrow.' One could say that she was noting the absence of psychosomatic climax.[5] The patient went on to say that she has been organizing the weekend as much as possible, but she is usually unable to distinguish between fantasying, which paralyses action, and real planning, which has to do with looking forward to action. There is an enormous amount of distress because of the neglect of her immediate environment following the paralysis of action from which she suffers.

At a school concert the children sang 'The skies will shine in splendour' exactly as she in school sang it forty-five years ago, and she was wondering whether some of the children would be

---

[5] Another aspect of this type of experience I have discussed in terms of the capacity for ego orgasm (Winnicott, 1958b).

like her, not knowing about the skies shining because eternally engaged in some form of fantasying.

We came round in the end to a discussion of this dream that she had reported at the beginning (cutting out a dress) which was experienced while she was awake and was a defence against dreaming: 'But how is she to know?' Fantasying possesses her like an evil spirit. From here she went on to her great need to be able to possess herself and to be in possession and to be in control. Suddenly she became tremendously aware of the fact that this fantasying was not a dream and I could see from this that she had not been fully aware of this fact previously. It was like this: she woke, and there she was madly making a dress. It was like saying to me: 'You think I can dream. Well, you are mistaken!' From here I was able to go to the dream equivalent, a dream of dressmaking. Perhaps for the first time I felt I could formulate the difference between dreaming and fantasying in the context of her therapy.

The fantasying is simply about making a dress. The dress has no symbolic value. A dog is a dog is a dog. In the dream, by contrast, as I was able to show with her help, the same thing would indeed have had symbolic meaning. We looked at this.

The area of formlessness

The key word to be carried back into the dream was formlessness, which is what the material is like before it is patterned and cut and shaped and put together. In other words, in a dream this would be a comment on her own personality and self-establishment. In a dream it would only to some extent be about a dress. Moreover, the hope that would make her feel that something could be made out of the formlessness would then come from the confidence that she had in her analyst, who has to counteract all that she carries forward from her childhood. Her childhood environment seemed unable to allow her to be formless but must, as she felt it, pattern her and cut her out into shapes conceived by other people.[6]

At the very end of the session she had a moment of intense feeling associated with the idea that there had been no one (from her point of view) in her childhood who had understood that she had to begin in formlessness. As she reached recognition of this she became very angry indeed. If any therapeutic result came from this session it would be chiefly derived from her having arrived at this intense anger, anger that was about something, not mad, but with logical motivation.

At the next visit, another two-hour session, the patient reported to me that since the last visit she had done a very great deal. She was of course alarmed to have to report what I might take as implying progress. She felt that the key word was identity. A great deal of the first part of this long session was taken up with describing her activities, which included clearing up messes that had been left for months or even years, and also constructive work. Undoubtedly she had enjoyed a great deal of what she did. All the time, however, she was showing a great fear of loss of identity as if it might turn out that she had been so patterned, and that the whole thing was playing at being grown-up; or playing at making progress for the analyst's sake along the lines laid down by the analyst.

The day was hot and the patient was tired and she lay back in the chair and went to sleep. She had on a dress that she had been able to make wearable both for work and for coming to me. She slept for about ten minutes. When she woke she continued with her doubts about the validity of what she had actually done at home and even enjoyed. The important thing arising out of the sleep was that she felt it was a failure because she did not

[6] This can be seen, then, in terms of compliance and a false self organization (cf. Winnicott, 1960a).

remember the dreams. It was as if she had gone to sleep in order to have a dream for the analysis. It was a relief to her when I pointed out that she went to sleep because she wanted to go to sleep. I said that dreaming is just something that happens when you are asleep. Now she felt that the sleep had done her a great deal of good. She wanted to go to sleep and when she woke up she felt much more real and somehow not remembering any dreams no longer mattered. She spoke about the way when your eyes go out of focus you know things are there but you don't quite see them, and how her mind is like that. It is out of focus. I said: 'But in the dreaming that accompanies sleep the mind is out of focus because it is not focusing on anything unless coming round to the sort of dream that can be brought forward into waking life and reported.' I had in mind the word 'formlessness' from the last session, and I was applying it to generalized dream activity, as contrasted with dreaming.[7]

In the remainder of the session a great deal happened because the patient felt real and she was working at her problem with me her analyst. She gave a very good example of a tremendous lot happening all of a sudden in fantasying which was of the kind that paralyses action. I took this now as the clue that she could give me towards the understanding of dream. The *fantasy* had to do with some people coming and taking over her flat. That is all. The *dream* that people came and took over her flat would have to do with her finding new possibilities in her own personality and also with the enjoyment of identifications with other people, including her parents. This is the opposite of feeling patterned and gives her a way of identifying without loss of identity. To support my interpretation I found a language which was suitable through knowing the patient's great interest in poetry. I said that fantasying was about a

---

[7] One would expect a different EEG effect from these two extremes, according to which is dominant in any one phase.

certain subject and it was a dead end. It *had no poetic value*. The corresponding dream, however, *had poetry in it*, that is to say, layer upon layer of meaning related to past, present, and future, and to inner and outer, and always fundamentally about herself. It is this poetry of the dream that is missing in her fantasying and in this way it is impossible for me to give meaningful interpretations about fantasying. I do not even try to use the material of fantasying that children in the latency period can supply in any quantity.

The patient went over the work that we had done with deeper recognition and understanding, especially feeling the symbolism in the dream which is absent in the limited area of fantasying.

She then made some excursions into imaginative planning of the future which seemed to give a prospect of future happiness that was different from the here-and-now fixity of any satisfaction that there can be in fantasying. All the time I needed to be extremely careful, and I pointed this out to her, lest I appeared to be pleased with her for all that she had done and the big change that had occurred in her; so easily she would have the feeling that she had fitted in and been patterned by me, and this would be followed by maximal protest and a return to the fixity of fantasying, playing patience and the other related routines.

Then a thought came to her and she said: 'What was last time about?' (It is characteristic of this patient that she does not remember the previous session although often she is obviously affected by it, as in this case.) I had the word 'formlessness' ready and from this she got back to the whole previous session and to the idea of the dress material before it was cut out and the feeling that nobody had ever recognized her need to start from formlessness. She repeated that she was tired today and I pointed out that this was something, not nothing. To some extent it is being in control: 'I am tired, I am going to sleep.' She had the same feeling in her car. She was tired but she did not go to sleep because she was driving. Here, however, she could go to sleep. Suddenly she saw a possibility of health and found it breath-taking. She used the words: 'I might be able to be in charge of myself. To be in control, to use imagination with discretion.'

There was one more thing to be done in this long session. She brought up the subject of playing patience, which she called a quagmire, and asked for help in regard to the understanding of it. Using what we had done together, I was able to say that patience is a form of fantasying, is a dead end, and cannot be used by me. If on the other hand she is telling me a dream – 'I dreamt I was playing patience' – then I could use it, and indeed I could make an interpretation. I could say: 'You are struggling with God or fate, sometimes winning and sometimes losing, the aim being to control the destinies of four royal families.' She was able to follow on from this without help and her comment afterwards was: 'I have been playing patience for hours in my empty room and the room really is empty because while I am playing patience I do not exist.' Here again she said: 'So I might become interested in me.'

At the end she was reluctant to go, not as on the previous recent occasion because of sadness at leaving the only person she can discuss things with, but chiefly on this occasion because going home she might find herself less ill – that is to say, less rigidly fixed in a defence organization. Now, instead of being able to predict everything that will happen, she cannot any longer tell whether she will go home and do something she wanted to do or whether playing patience will possess her. It was clear that she had nostalgia for the certainty of the illness pattern and great anxiety about the uncertainty that goes with the freedom to choose.

It did seem to me at the end of this session that one could claim that the work of the previous session had had a profound effect.

On the other hand, I was only too aware of the great danger of becoming confident or even pleased. The analyst's neutrality was needed here if anywhere in the whole treatment. In this kind of work we know that we are always starting again, and the less we expect the better.

3

PLAYING

A theoretical statement

In this chapter I am trying to explore an idea that has been forced on me by my work, and also forced on me by my own stage of development at the present time, which gives my work a certain colouring. I need not say that my work, which is largely psychoanalysis, also includes psychotherapy, and for the purpose of this chapter I do not need to draw a clear distinction between the uses of the two terms.

When I come to state my thesis I find, as so often, that it is very simple, and that not many words are needed to cover the subject. *Psychotherapy takes place in the overlap of two areas of playing, that of the patient and that of the therapist. Psychotherapy has to do with two people playing together. The corollary of this is that where playing is not possible then the work done by the therapist is directed towards bringing the patient from a state of not being able to play into a state of being able to play.*

Although I am not attempting to review the literature I do wish to pay tribute to the work of Milner (1952, 1957, 1969), who has written brilliantly on the subject of symbol-formation. However, I shall not let her deep comprehensive study stop me from drawing attention to the subject of playing in my own words. Milner (1952) relates children's playing to concentration in adults:

> 'When I began to see . . . that this use of me might be not only a defensive regression, but an essential recurrent phase of a creative relation to the world . . .'

Milner was referring to a *prelogical fusion of subject and object*. I am trying to distinguish between this fusion and the fusion or defusion of the subjective object and the object objectively perceived.[1] I believe that what I am attempting to do is also inherent in the material of Milner's contribution. Here is another of her statements:

> 'Moments when the original poet in each of us created the outside world for us, by finding the familiar in the unfamiliar, are perhaps forgotten by most people; or else they are guarded in some secret place of memory because they were too much like visitations of the gods to be mixed with everyday thinking' (Milner, 1957).

Play and masturbation

There is one thing that I want to get out of the way. In psycho-analytic writings and discussions, the subject of playing has been

---

[1] For further discussion of this the reader may consult my papers 'Ego Integration in Child Development' (1962) and 'Communicating and Not Communicating leading to a Study of Certain Opposites' (1963a).

too closely linked with masturbation and the various sensuous experiences. It is true that when we are confronted with masturbation we always think: what is the fantasy? And it is also true that when we witness playing we tend to wonder what is the physical excitement that is linked with the type of play that we witness. But playing needs to be studied as a subject on its own, supplementary to the concept of the sublimation of instinct.

It may very well be that we have missed something by having these two phenomena (playing and masturbatory activity) so closely linked in our minds. I have tried to point out that when a child is playing the masturbatory element is essentially lacking; or, in other words, that if when a child is playing the physical excitement of instinctual involvement becomes evident, then the playing stops, or is at any rate spoiled (Winnicott, 1968a). Both Kris (1951) and Spitz (1962) have enlarged the concept of auto-erotism to cover data of a similar kind (also cf. Khan, 1964).

I am reaching towards a new statement of playing, and it interests me when I seem to see in the psychoanalytic literature the lack of a useful statement on the subject of play. Child analysis of whatever school is built around the child's playing, and it would be rather strange if we were to find that in order to get a good statement about playing we have to go to those who have written on the subject who are not analysts (e.g. Lowenfeld, 1935).

Naturally one turns to the work of Melanie Klein (1932), but I suggest that in her writings Klein, in so far as she was concerned with play, was concerned almost entirely with the use of play. The therapist is reaching for the child's communication and knows that the child does not usually possess the command of language that can convey the infinite subtleties that are to be found in play by those who seek. This is not a criticism of Melanie Klein or of others who have described the use of a child's play in the psychoanalysis of children. It is simply a comment on the possibility that in the total theory of the personality the psychoanalyst has been too busy using play content to look at the playing child, and to write about playing as a thing in itself. It is obvious that I am making a significant distinction between the meanings of the noun 'play' and the verbal noun 'playing'.

Whatever I say about children playing really applies to adults as well, only the matter is more difficult to describe when the patient's material appears mainly in terms of verbal communication. I suggest that we must expect to find playing just as evident in the analyses of adults as it is in the case of our work with children. It manifests itself, for instance, in the choice of words, in the inflections of the voice, and indeed in the sense of humour.

Transitional phenomena

For me the meaning of playing has taken on a new colour since I have followed up the theme of transitional phenomena, tracing these in all their subtle developments right from the early use of a transitional object or technique to the ultimate stages of a human being's capacity for cultural experience.

I think it is not out of place to draw attention here to the generosity that has been shown in psychoanalytic circles and in the general psychiatric world in respect of my description of transitional phenomena. I am interested in the fact that right through the field of child care this idea has caught on, and sometimes I feel that I have been given more than my due reward in this area. What I called transitional phenomena are universal and it was simply a matter of drawing attention to them and to their potential for use in the building of theory. Wulff (1946) had already, as I discovered, written about fetish objects employed by babies or children, and I know that in Anna Freud's psychotherapy clinic these objects have been observed with small children. I have heard Anna Freud speak of the use of the talisman, a closely allied phenomenon (cf. A. Freud, 1965). A. A. Milne, of course, immortalized Winnie the Pooh. Schulz and Arthur Miller,[2] among other authors, have drawn on these objects that I have specifically referred to and named.

I am encouraged by the happy fate of the concept of transitional phenomena to think that what I am trying to say now about playing may also be readily acceptable. There is something about playing that has not yet found a place in the psychoanalytic literature.

In the chapter on cultural experience and its location (Chapter 7) I make my idea of play concrete by claiming that *playing has a place* and a time. It is not *inside* by any use of the word (and it is unfortunately true that the word inside has very many and various uses in psychoanalytic discussion). Nor is it *outside*, that is to say, it is not a part of the repudiated world, the not-me, that which the individual has decided to recognize (with whatever difficulty and even pain) as truly external, which is outside magical control. To control what is outside one has to *do* things, not simply to think or to wish, and *doing things takes* time. Playing is doing.

Playing in time and space

In order to give a place to playing I postulated a *potential space* between the baby and the mother. This potential space varies a very great deal according to the life experiences of the baby in relation to the mother or mother-figure, and I contrast this potential space (*a*) with the inner world (which is related to the psychosomatic partnership) and (*b*) with actual, or external, reality (which has its own dimensions, and which can be studied objectively, and which, however much it may seem to vary

---

[2] Miller (1963): This story does eventually tail off into a sentimental ending, and therefore, as it seems to me, abandons the direct link with childhood observation.

according to the state of the individual who is observing it, does in fact remain constant).

I can now restate what I am trying to convey. I want to draw attention away from the sequence psychoanalysis, psychotherapy, play material, playing, and to set this up again the other way round. In other words, it is play that is the universal, and that belongs to health: playing facilitates growth and therefore health; playing leads into group relationships; playing can be a form of communication in psychotherapy; and, lastly, psychoanalysis has been developed as a highly specialized form of playing in the service of communication with oneself and others.

The natural thing is playing, and the highly sophisticated twentieth-century phenomenon is psychoanalysis. It must be of value to the analyst to be constantly reminded not only of what is owed to Freud but also of what we owe to the natural and universal thing called playing.

It is hardly necessary to illustrate something so obvious as playing; nevertheless I propose to give two examples.

Edmund, Aged Two and a Half Years

The mother came to consult me about herself and she brought Edmund with her. Edmund was in my room while I was talking to his mother, and I placed among us a table and a little chair which he could use if he wished to do so. He looked serious but not frightened or depressed. He said: 'Where's toys?' This is all he said throughout the hour. Evidently he had been told to expect toys and I said that there were some to be found at the other end of the room on the floor under the bookcase.

Soon he fetched a bucketful of toys and he was playing in a deliberate way while the consultation between the mother and me proceeded. The mother was able to tell me the exact significant moment at two years five months when Edmund had started stammering, after which he gave up talking 'because the stammer frightened him'. While she and I were going through with a consultation situation about herself and about him, Edmund placed some small train parts on the table and was arranging them and making them join up and relate. He was only two feet away from his mother. Soon he got onto her lap and had a short spell as a baby. She responded naturally and adequately. Then he got down spontaneously and took up playing again at the table. All this happened while his mother and I were heavily engaged in deep conversation.

After about twenty minutes Edmund began to liven up, and he went to the other end of the room for a fresh supply of toys. Out of the muddle there he brought a tangle of string. The mother (undoubtedly affected by his choice of string, but not conscious of the symbolism) made the remark: At his most non-verbal Edmund is most clinging, needing contact with my *actual* breast, and needing my *actual* lap.' At the time when the stammer began he had been starting to comply, but he had reverted to incontinence along with the stammer, and this was followed by abandonment of talking. He was beginning to cooperate again at about the time of the consultation. The mother saw this as being part of a recovery from a setback in his development.

By taking notice of Edmund's playing I was able to maintain communication with the mother.

Now Edmund developed a bubble in his mouth while playing with the toys. He became preoccupied with the string. The mother made the comment that as a baby he refused all except the breast, till he grew up and went over to a cup. 'He brooks no substitute', she said, meaning that he would not take from a baby's bottle, and a refusal of substitutes had become a permanent feature in his character. Even his mother's mother, of whom he is fond, is not fully accepted because she is not the actual mother. All his life he has had his mother herself to settle him at night. There were breast troubles when he was born, and he used to cling on with his gums in the first days and weeks, perhaps as an insurance against mother's sensitive protection of herself, she being in a tender state. At ten months he had a tooth, and on one occasion he bit, but this did not draw blood.

'He was not quite so easy a baby as the first had been.'

All this took time, and was mixed up with the other matters that the mother wished to discuss with me. Edmund seemed here to be concerned with the one end of the string that was exposed, the rest of the string being in a tangle. Sometimes he would make a gesture which was as if he 'plugged in' with the end of the string like an electric flex to his mother's thigh. One had to observe that although he 'brooked no substitute' he was using the string as a symbol of union with his mother. It was clear that the string was simultaneously a symbol of separateness and of union through communication.

The mother told me that he had had a transitional object called 'my blanket' – he could use any blanket that had a satin binding like the binding of the original one of his early infancy.

At this point Edmund quite naturally left the toys, got onto the couch and crept like an animal towards his mother and curled up on her lap. He stayed there about three minutes. She gave a very natural response, not exaggerated. Then he uncurled and returned to the toys. He now put the string (which he seemed fond of) at the bottom of the bucket like bedding, and began to put the toys in, so that they had a nice soft place to lie in, like a cradle or cot. After once more clinging to his mother and then returning to the toys, he was ready to go, the mother and I having finished our business.

In this play he had illustrated much of that which the mother was talking about (although she was also talking about herself). He had communicated an ebb and flow of movement in him away from and back to dependence. But this was not psychotherapy since I was working with the mother. What Edmund did was simply to display the ideas that occupied his life while his mother and I were talking together. I did not interpret and I must assume that this child would have been liable to play just like this without there being anyone there to see or to receive the communication, in which case it would perhaps have been a communication with some part of the self, the observing ego. As it happened I was there mirroring what was taking place and thus giving it a quality of communication (cf. Winnicott, 1967b).

Diana, Aged Five Years

In the second case, as with the case of Edmund, I had to conduct two consultations in parallel, one with the mother, who was in distress, and a play relationship with the daughter Diana. She had a little brother (at home) who was mentally defective and who had a congenital deformity of the heart. The mother came to discuss the effect of this brother on herself and on her daughter Diana.

My contact with the mother lasted an hour. The child was with us all the time, and my task was a threefold one: to give the mother full attention because of her own needs, to play with the child, and (for the purpose of writing this paper) to record the nature of Diana's play.

As a matter of fact it was Diana herself who took charge from the beginning, for as I opened the front door to let in the mother an eager little girl presented herself, putting forward a small teddy. I did not look at her mother or at her, but I went straight for the teddy and said: 'What's his name?' She said: 'Just Teddy.' So a strong relationship between Diana and myself had quickly developed, and I needed to keep this going in order to do my main job, which was to meet the needs of the mother. In the consulting-room Diana needed all the time, naturally, to feel that she had my attention, but it was possible for me to give the mother the attention she needed and to play with Diana too.

In describing this case, as in describing the case of Edmund, I shall give what happened between me and Diana, leaving out the material of the consultation with the mother.

When we all three got into the consulting-room we settled down, the mother sitting on the couch, Diana having a small chair to herself near the child table. Diana took her small teddy bear and stuffed it into my breast pocket. She tried to see how far it would go down, and examined the lining of my jacket, and from this she became interested in the various pockets and the way that they did not communicate with each other. This was happening while the mother and I were talking seriously about the backward child of two and a half, and Diana gave the additional information: 'He has a hole in his heart.' One could say that while playing she was listening with one ear. It seemed to me that she was able to accept her brother's physical disability due to the hole in his heart while not finding his mental backwardness within her range.

In the playing that Diana and I did together, playing without therapeutics in it, I felt free to be playful. Children play more easily when the other person is able and free to be playful. I suddenly put my ear to the teddy bear in my pocket and I said: 'I heard him say something!' She was very interested in this. I said: 'I think he wants someone to play with', and I told her about the woolly lamb that she would find if she looked at the other end of the room in the mess of toys under the shelf. Perhaps I had an ulterior motive which was to get the bear out of my pocket. Diana went and fetched the lamb, which was considerably bigger than the bear, and she took up my idea of friendship between the teddy bear and the lamb. For some time she put the teddy and the lamb together on the couch near where the mother was sitting. I of course was continuing my interview with the mother, and it could be noted that Diana retained an interest in what we were saying, doing this with some part of herself, a part that identifies with grown-ups and grown-up attitudes.

In the play Diana decided that these two creatures were her children. She put them up under her clothes, making herself pregnant with them. After a period of pregnancy she announced they were going to be born, but they were 'not going to be twins'. She made it very evident that the lamb was to be born first and then the teddy bear. After the birth was complete she put her two newly born children together on a bed which she improvised on the floor, and she covered them up. At first she put one at one end and the other at the other end, saying that if they were together they would fight. They might 'meet in the middle of the bed under the clothes and fight'. Then she put them sleeping together peacefully, at the top of the improvised bed. She now went and fetched a lot of toys in a bucket and in some boxes. On the floor around the top end of the bed she arranged the toys and played with them; the playing was orderly and there were several different themes that developed, each kept separate from the other. I came in again with an idea of my own. I said: 'Oh look! you are putting on the floor around these babies' heads the dreams that they are having while they are asleep.' This idea intrigued her and she took it up and went on developing the various themes as if dreaming their dreams for the babies. All this was giving the mother and me time which we badly needed because of the work we were doing together. Somewhere just here the mother was crying and was very disturbed and Diana looked up for a moment prepared to be anxious. I said to her: 'Mother is crying because she is thinking of your brother who is ill. 'This reassured Diana because it was direct and factual, and she said 'hole in the heart' and then continued dreaming the babies' dreams for them.

So here was Diana not coming for a consultation about herself and not being in any special need of help, playing with me and on her own, and at the same time caught up in her mother's state. I could see that the mother had needed to bring Diana, she being herself too anxious for a direct confrontation with myself because of the very deep disturbance she felt on account of having an ill boy. Later, the mother came to me by herself, no longer needing the distraction of the child.

When at a later date I saw the mother alone we were able to go over what happened when I saw her with Diana, and the mother was then able to add this important detail, that Diana's father exploits Diana's forwardness and likes her best when she is just like a little grown-up. There can be seen in the material a pull towards premature ego development, an identification with the mother and a participation in the mother's problems that arise out of the fact that the brother is actually ill and abnormal.

Looking back on what happened I find it possible to say that Diana had prepared herself before she set out to come, although the interview was not arranged for her benefit. From what the mother told me I could see that Diana was organized for the contact with me just as if she knew she was coming to a psychotherapist. Before starting out she had collected together the first of her teddy bears and also her discarded transitional object. She did not bring the latter but came prepared to organize a somewhat regressive experience in her play activities. At the same time the mother and I were witnessing Diana's ability to be identified with her mother not only in respect of the pregnancy but also in respect of taking responsibility for the management of the brother.

Here, as with Edmund, the play was of a self-healing kind. In each case the result was comparable with a psychotherapeutic session in which the story would have been punctuated by interpretations from the therapist. A psychotherapist might perhaps have refrained from actively playing with Diana, as when I said I heard the teddy say something, and when I said what I said about Diana's children's dreams being played out on the floor. But this self-imposed discipline might have eliminated some of the creative aspect of Diana's play experience.

I choose these two examples simply because these were two consecutive cases in my practice that came one morning when I was engaged in the writing of the paper on which this chapter is based.

THEORY OF PLAY

It is possible to describe a sequence of relationships related to the developmental process and to look and see where playing belongs.

A. Baby and object are merged in with one another. Baby's view of the object is subjective and the mother is oriented towards the making actual of what the baby is ready to find.

B. The object is repudiated, re-accepted, and perceived object-ively. This complex process is highly dependent on there being a mother or mother-figure prepared to participate and to give back what is handed out.

This means that the mother (or part of mother) is in a 'to and fro' between being that which the baby has a capacity to find and (alternatively) being herself waiting to be found.

If the mother can play this part over a length of time without admitting impediment (so to speak) then the baby has some *experience* of magical control, that is, experience of that which is called 'omnipotence' in the description of intrapsychic processes (cf. Winnicott, 1962).

In the state of confidence that grows up when a mother can do this difficult thing well (not if she is unable to do it), the baby begins to enjoy experiences based on a 'marriage' of the omnipotence of intrapsychic processes with the baby's control of the actual. Confidence in the mother makes an intermediate playground here, where the idea of magic originates, since the baby does to some extent *experience* omnipotence. All this bears closely on Erikson's work on identity-formation (Erikson, 1956). I call this a playground because play starts here. The playground is a potential space between the mother and the baby or joining mother and baby.

Play is immensely exciting. It is exciting not primarily because the instincts are involved, be it understood! The thing about playing is always the precariousness of the interplay of personal psychic reality and the experience of control of actual objects. This is the precariousness of magic itself, magic that arises in intimacy, in a relationship that is being found to be reliable. To be reliable the relationship is necessarily motivated by the mother's love, or her love-hate, or her object-relating, not by reaction-formations. When a patient cannot play the therapist must attend to this major symptom before interpreting fragments of behaviour.

C. The next stage is being alone in the presence of someone. The child is now playing on the basis of the assumption that the person who loves and who is therefore reliable is available and continues to be available when remembered after being forgotten. This person is felt to reflect back what happens in the playing.[3]
D. The child is now getting ready for the next stage, which is to allow and to enjoy an overlap of two play areas. First, surely, it is the mother who plays with the baby, but she is rather careful to fit in with the baby's play activities. Sooner or later, however, she introduces her own playing, and she finds that babies vary according to their capacity to like or dislike the introduction of ideas that are not their own.

Thus the way is paved for a playing together in a relationship.

As I look back over the papers that mark the development of my own thought and understanding I can see that my present inter-

[3] I have discussed a more sophisticated aspect of these experiences in my paper 'The Capacity to be Alone' (1958b).

est in play in the relationship of trust that may develop between the baby and the mother was always a feature of my consultative technique, as the following example from my first book shows (Winnicott, 1931). And further, ten years later, I was to elaborate on it in my paper 'The Observation of Infants in a Set Situation' (Winnicott, 1941).

Illustrative Case

A girl first attended hospital when six months old, with moderately severe infective gastro-enteritis. She was the first baby, breast-fed. She had a tendency to constipation till six months, but not after.

At seven months she was brought again because she began to lie awake, crying. She was sick after food, and did not enjoy the breast feeds. Supplementary feeds had to be given and weaning was completed in a few weeks.

At nine months she had a fit, and continued to have occasional fits, usually at 5 a.m., about a quarter of an hour after waking. The fits affected both sides and lasted five minutes.

At eleven months the fits were frequent. The mother found she could prevent individual fits by distracting the child's attention. In one day she had to do this four times. The child had become nervy, jumping at the least sound. She had one fit in her sleep. In some of the fits she bit her tongue, and in some she was incontinent of urine.

At one year she was having four to five a day. It was noticed she would sometimes sit down after a feed, double up, and go off. She was given orange juice, then went off. She was put to sit on the floor, and a fit started. One morning she woke and immediately had a fit, then slept; soon she woke again and had another fit. At this time the fits began to be followed by a desire to sleep, but even at this severe stage the mother could often stop a fit in the early stage by distracting the child's attention. I made at the time this note:

> 'Taken on my knees she cries incessantly, but does not show hostility. She pulls my tie about in a careless way as she cries. Given back to her mother she shows no interest in the change and continues to cry, crying more and more pitifully right on through being dressed, and so till carried out of the building.'

At this time I witnessed a fit, which was marked by tonic and clonic stages and followed by sleep. The child was having four to five a day, and was crying all day, though sleeping at night.

Careful examinations revealed no sign of physical disease. Bromide was given in the day, according to need.

At one consultation I had the child on my knee observing her. She made a furtive attempt to bite my knuckle. Three days later I had her again on my knee, and waited to see what she would do. She bit my knuckle three times so severely that the skin was nearly torn. She then played at throwing spatulas on the floor incessantly for fifteen minutes. All the time she cried as if really unhappy. Two days later I had her on my knee for half an hour. She had had four convulsions in the previous two days. At first she cried as usual. She again bit my knuckle very severely, this time without showing guilt feelings, and then played the game of biting and throwing away spatulas; *while on my knee she became able to enjoy play*. After a while she began to finger her toes, and so I had her shoes and socks removed. The result of this was a period of experimentation which absorbed her whole interest. It looked as if she was discovering and proving over and over again, to her great satisfaction, that whereas spatulas can be put to the mouth, thrown away and lost, toes cannot be pulled off.

Four days later the mother came and said that since the last consultation the baby had been 'a different child'. She had not only had no fits, but had been sleeping well at night – happy all day, taking no bromide. Eleven days later the improvement had been maintained, without medicine; there had been no fits for fourteen days, and the mother asked to be discharged.

I visited this child one year later and found that since the last consultation she had had no symptom whatever. I found an entirely healthy, happy, intelligent and friendly child, fond of play, and free from the common anxieties.

Psychotherapy

Here in this area of overlap between the playing of the child and the playing of the other person there is a chance to introduce enrichments. The teacher aims at enrichment. By contrast, the therapist is concerned specifically with the child's own growth processes, and with the removal of blocks to development that may have become evident. It is psychoanalytic theory that has made for an understanding of these blocks. At the same time it would be a narrow view to suppose that psychoanalysis is the only way to make therapeutic use of the child's playing.

It is good to remember always that playing is itself a therapy. To arrange for children to be able to play is itself a psychotherapy that has immediate and universal application, and it includes the establishment of a positive social attitude towards playing. This attitude must include recognition that playing is always liable to become frightening. Games and their organization must be looked at as part of an attempt to forestall the frightening aspect of playing. Responsible persons must be available when children play; but this does not mean that the responsible person need enter into the children's playing. When an organizer must be involved in a managerial position then the implication is that the child or the children are unable to play in the creative sense of my meaning in this communication.

The essential feature of my communication is this, that playing is an experience, always a creative experience, and it is an experience in the space-time continuum, a basic form of living.

The precariousness of play belongs to the fact that it is always on the theoretical line between the subjective and that which is objectively perceived.

It is my purpose here simply to give a reminder that children's playing has everything in it, although the psychotherapist works on the material, the content of playing. Naturally, in a set or professional hour a more precise constellation presents than would present in a timeless experience on the floor at home (cf. Winnicott, 1941); but it helps us to understand our work if we know that the basis of what we do is the patient's playing, a creative experience taking up space and time, and intensely real for the patient.

Also, this observation helps us to understand how it is that psychotherapy of a deep-going kind may be done without interpretative work. A good example of this is the work of Axline (1947) of New York. Her work on psychotherapy is of great importance to us. I appreciate Axline's work in a special way because it joins up with the point that I make in reporting what I call 'therapeutic consultations', that the significant moment is that at which the child surprises himself or herself. It is not the moment of my clever interpretation that is significant (Winnicott, 1971).

Interpretation outside the ripeness of the material is indoctrination and produces compliance (Winnicott, 1960a). A corollary is that resistance arises out of interpretation given out-side the area of the overlap of the patient's and the analyst's playing together. Interpretation when the patient has no capacity to play is simply not useful, or causes confusion. When there is mutual playing, then interpretation according to accepted psychoanalytic principles can carry the therapeutic work forward. This playing has to be spontaneous, and not compliant or acquiescent, if psychotherapy is to be done.

Summary

(a) To get to the idea of playing it is helpful to think of the *preoccupation* that characterizes the playing of a young child. The content does not matter. What matters is the near-withdrawal state, akin to the *concentration* of older children and adults. The playing child inhabits an area that cannot be easily left, nor can it easily admit intrusions.

(b) This area of playing is not inner psychic reality. It is outside the individual, but it is not the external world.

(c) Into this play area the child gathers objects or phenomena from external reality and uses these in the service of some sample derived from inner or personal reality. Without hallucinating the child puts out a sample of dream potential and lives with this sample in a chosen setting of fragments from external reality.

(d) In playing, the child manipulates external phenomena in the service of the dream and invests chosen external phenomena with dream meaning and feeling.

(e) There is a direct development from transitional phenomena to playing, and from playing to shared playing, and from this to cultural experiences.

(f) Playing implies trust, and belongs to the potential space between (what was at first) baby and mother-figure, with the baby in a state of near-absolute dependence, and the mother-figure's adaptive function taken for granted by the baby.

(g) Playing involves the body:
  (i) because of the manipulation of objects;
  (ii) because certain types of intense interest are associated with certain aspects of bodily excitement.

(h) Bodily excitement in erotogenic zones constantly threatens playing, and therefore threatens the child's sense of existing as a person. The instincts are the main threat to play as to the ego; in seduction some external agency exploits the child's instincts and helps to annihilate the child's sense of existing as an autonomous unit, making playing impossible (cf. Khan, 1964).

(i) *Playing is essentially satisfying*. This is true even when it leads to a high degree of anxiety. There is a degree of anxiety that is unbearable and this destroys playing.

(j) The pleasurable element in playing carries with it the implication that the instinctual arousal is not excessive; instinctual arousal beyond a certain point must lead to:

    (i) climax;

    (ii) failed climax and a sense of mental confusion and physical discomfort that only time can mend;

    (iii) alternative climax (as in provocation of parental or social reaction, anger, etc.).

Playing can be said to reach its own saturation point, which refers to the capacity to contain experience.

(k) Playing is inherently exciting and precarious. This characteristic derives not from instinctual arousal but from the precariousness that belongs to the interplay in the child's mind of that which is subjective (near-hallucination) and that which is objectively perceived (actual, or shared reality).

4

PLAYING

Creative activity and the search for the self

Now I shall discuss an important feature of playing. This is that in playing, and perhaps only in playing, the child or adult is free to be creative. This consideration arises in my mind as a development of the concept of transitional phenomena and it takes into account the difficult part of the theory of the transitional object, which is that a paradox is involved which needs to be accepted, tolerated, and not resolved.

A further detail of theory that has importance here is described as having to do with the location of playing, a theme I have developed in Chapters 3, 7, and 8. The important part of this concept is that whereas inner psychic reality has a kind of location in the mind or in the belly or in the head or somewhere within the bounds of the individual's personality, and whereas what is called external reality is located outside those bounds, playing and cultural experience can be given a location if one uses the concept of the potential space between the mother and the baby. In the development of various individuals, it has to be recognized that the third area of potential space between mother and baby is extremely valuable according to the experiences of the child or adult who is being considered. I have referred to these ideas again in Chapter 5, where I draw attention to the fact that a description of the emotional development of the individual cannot be made entirely in terms of the individual, but that in certain areas, and this is one of them, perhaps the main one, the behaviour of the environment is part of the individual's own personal development and must therefore be included. As a psychoanalyst I find that these ideas affect what I do as an analyst without, as I believe, altering my adherence to the important features of psychoanalysis that we teach our students and that provide a common factor in the teaching of psychoanalysis as we believe it to be derived from the work of Freud.

I am not involved by deliberate intention in the comparison of psychotherapy with psychoanalysis or indeed in any attempt to define these two processes in such a way that would show up a clear line of demarcation between the two. The general principle seems to me to be valid that *psychotherapy is done in the overlap of the two play areas, that of the patient and that of the therapist.* If the therapist cannot play, then he is not suitable for the work. If the patient cannot play, then something needs to be done to enable the patient to become able to play, after which psychotherapy may begin. The reason why playing is essential is that it is in playing that the patient is being creative.

THE SEARCH FOR THE SELF

In this chapter I am concerned with the search for the self and the restatement of the fact that certain conditions are necessary if success is to be achieved in this search. These conditions are associated with what is usually called creativity. It is in playing and only in playing that the individual child or adult is able to be creative and to use the whole personality, and it is only in being creative that the individual discovers the self.

(Bound up with this is the fact that only in playing is communication possible; except direct communication, which belongs to psychopathology or to an extreme of immaturity.

It is a frequent experience in clinical work to meet with persons who want help and who are searching for the self and who are trying to find themselves in the products of their creative experiences. But to help these patients we must know about creativity itself. It is as if we are looking at a baby in the early stages and jumping forward to the child who takes faeces or some substance with the texture of faeces and tries to make something out of the substance. This kind of creativity is valid and well understood, but a separate study is needed of creativity as a feature of life and total living. I am suggesting that the search for the self in terms of what can be done with waste products is a search that is doomed to be never-ending and essentially unsuccessful.

In a search for the self the person concerned may have produced something valuable in terms of art, but a successful artist may be universally acclaimed and yet have failed to find the self that he or she is looking for. The self is not really to be found in what is made out of products of body or mind, however valuable these constructs may be in terms of beauty, skill, and impact. If the artist (in whatever medium) is searching for the self, then it can be said that in all probability there is already some failure for that artist in the field of general creative living. The finished creation never heals the underlying lack of sense of self.

Before developing this idea further I must state a second theme, one that is related to the first but needs separate treatment. This second theme is that the person we are trying to help might expect to feel cured when we explain. The person might say: 'I see what you mean; I am myself when I feel creative and when I make a creative gesture, and now the search is ended.' In practice this does not seem to be a description of what happens. In this kind of work we know that even the right explanation is ineffectual. The person we are trying to help needs a new experience in a specialized setting. The experience is one of a non-purposive state, as one might say a sort of ticking over of the unintegrated personality. I referred to this as formlessness in the case description (Chapter 2).

Account has to be taken of the reliability or unreliability of the setting in which the individual is operating. We are brought up against a need for a differentiation between purposive activity and the alternative of non-purposive being. This relates to Balint's (1968) formulation of benign and malignant regression (see also Khan, 1969).

I am trying to refer to the essentials that make relaxation possible. In terms of free association this means that the patient on the couch or the child patient among the toys on the floor must be allowed to communicate a succession of ideas, thoughts, impulses, sensations that are not linked except in some way that is neurological or physiological and perhaps beyond detection. That is to say: it is where there is purpose or where there is anxiety or where there is lack of trust based on the need for defence that the analyst will be able to recognize and to point out the connection (or several connections) between the various components of free association material.

In the relaxation that belongs to trust and to acceptance of the professional reliability of the therapeutic setting (be it analytic, psychotherapeutic, social work, architectural, etc.), there is room for the idea of unrelated thought sequences which the analyst will do well to accept as such, not assuming the existence of a significant thread (cf. Milner, 1957, especially the appendix, pp. 148–163).

The contrast between these two related conditions can perhaps be illustrated if one thinks of a patient who is able to rest after work but *not able to achieve the resting state out of which a creative reaching-out can take place*. According to this theory, free association that reveals a coherent theme is already affected by anxiety, and the cohesion of ideas is a defence organization. Perhaps it is to be accepted that there are patients who at times need the therapist to note the nonsense that belongs to the mental state of the individual at rest without the need even for the patient to communicate this nonsense, that is to say, without the need for the patient to organize nonsense. Organized nonsense is already a defence, just as organized chaos is a denial of chaos. The therapist who cannot take this communication becomes engaged in a futile attempt to find some organization in the nonsense, as a result of which the patient leaves the nonsense area because of hopelessness about communicating nonsense. An opportunity for rest has been missed because of the therapist's need to find sense where nonsense is. The patient has been unable to rest because of a failure of the environmental provision, which undid the sense of trust. The therapist has, without knowing it, abandoned the professional role, and has done so by bending over backwards to be a clever analyst, and to see order in chaos.

It may be that these matters are reflected in the two kinds of sleep, sometimes denoted REM and NREM (rapid eye movements and no rapid eye movements).

In developing what I have to say I shall need the sequence:

(a) relaxation in conditions of trust based on experience;
(b) creative, physical, and mental activity manifested in play;
(c) the summation of these experiences forming the basis for a sense of self.

Summation or reverberation depends on there being a certain quantity of reflecting back to the individual on the part of the trusted therapist (or friend) who has taken the (indirect) communication. In these highly specialized conditions the individual can come together and exist as a unit, not as a defence against anxiety but as an expression of I AM, I am alive, I am myself (Winnicott, 1962). From this position everything is creative.

CASE IN ILLUSTRATION

I wish to use material from the record of a woman who is having treatment with me and who, as it happens, comes once a week. She had had a long treatment on a five-times-a-week basis for six years before coming to me, but found she needed a session of indefinite length, and this I could manage only once a week. We soon settled down to a session of three hours, later reduced to two hours.

If I can give a correct description of a session the reader will notice that over long periods I withhold interpretations, and often make no sound at all. This strict discipline has paid dividends. I have taken notes, because this helps me in a case seen only once a week, and I found that note-taking did not disrupt the work in this case. Also I often relieve my mind by writing down interpretations that I actually withhold. My reward for withholding interpretations comes when the patient makes the interpretation herself, perhaps an hour or two later.

My description amounts to a plea to every therapist to allow for the patient's capacity to play, that is, to be creative in the analytic work. The patient's creativity can be only too easily stolen by a therapist who knows too much. It does not really matter, of course, how much the therapist knows provided he can hide this knowledge, or refrain from advertising what he knows.

Let me try to convey the feeling of what it is like to do work with this patient. But I must ask the reader to exert patience, much as I needed to be patient when engaged in this work.

An example of a session

First, some life details, and arrangements of a practical nature – about sleep, spoilt when she gets het-up, books for sleep-making, a good one and a horrifying one; tired but het-up, so restless; rapid heart-beats, as now. Then, some difficulty about food: 'I want to be able to eat *when I feel hungry.*' (Food and books seem somehow equated in the substance of this desultory talking.)

'When you rang up, you knew, I hope, that I was too high' (elated).

I said: 'Yes, I suppose I did.'

Description of a phase of somewhat false improvement.

'But I knew I wasn't right.'

'It all seems so hopeful till I'm aware of it . . .'

'Depression and murderous feelings, that's me, and also it's me when I'm cheerful.'

> (*Half-hour gone*. The patient has been sitting in a low chair, or on the floor, or walking about.)

Long and slow description of positive and negative features of a walk she had taken.

'I don't seem able quite to BE – not me really looking – a screen – looking through glasses – imaginative looking isn't there. Is that just doctrine about the baby imagining the breast? In the previous treatment that I had there was an aeroplane overhead when I was on the way home from a session. I told the analyst next day that I suddenly imagined myself *being the aeroplane, flying high. Then it crashed to the ground.* The therapist said: "That's what happens to you when you project yourself into things and it makes an internal crash." '[1]

---

[1] I have no means of checking up on the accuracy of this report of the previous analyst's interpretation.

'Difficult to remember – I don't know if that's right – I don't really know what I want to say. It's as though there's just a mess inside, just a crash.'

(Three quarters of an hour had elapsed.)

She now became occupied with watching out of the window where she was standing, seeing a sparrow pecking away at a crust, suddenly 'taking a crumb away to its nest – or somewhere.' Then: 'Oh, I suddenly thought of a dream.'

The dream

'Some girl student kept bringing pictures that she had drawn. How could I tell her that these pictures show no improvement? I had thought that by letting myself be alone and meeting my depression . . . I'd better stop watching those sparrows – I can't think.'

(She was now on the floor with her head on a cushion on the chair.)

'I don't know . . . and yet you see there must be some sort of improvement.' (Details of her life given in illustration.) 'It's as though there isn't really a ME. Awful book of early teens called Returned Empty. That's what I feel like.'

(By now an hour had elapsed.)

She went on about the use of poetry – recited a poem of Christina Rosetti: 'Passing Away'.
'My life finishes with a canker in the bud.' Then to me: 'You've taken away my God!'

(Long pause.)

'I'm just spewing out on you anything that comes. I don't know what I've been talking about. I don't know . . . I dunno . . .'

(Long pause.)

(Looking out of the window again. Then five minutes of absolute quiet.)

'Just drifting like the clouds.'

(*About one and a half hours have passed now.*)

'You know I told you I did fingerpainting on the floor and how I got very frightened. I can't take up fingerpainting. I'm living in a mess. What am I to do? If I make myself read or paint is it any good? [Sighs.] I don't know . . . you see, in a way I don't like the mess on my hands in the fingerpainting.'

(Head now on cushion again.)

'I'm loath to come into this room.'

(Silence.)

'I dunno. I feel of no consequence.'
Odd details of examples of my manner of dealing with her, implying that she is of no consequence.
'I keep thinking that it may have been only ten minutes that cost me a lifetime.' (Reference to the original trauma not yet specified but all the time being worked out.)
'I suppose an injury would have to be repeated often for the effects to go so deep.'
Description of her view of her own childhood at various ages – how she tried all the time to feel of some consequence

by fitting in with what she thought was expected of her. Apt quotation from the poet Gerard Manley Hopkins.

(Long pause.)

'It's a desperate feeling of not mattering. I don't matter . . . there's no God and I don't matter. Imagine, a girl sent me a postcard from holiday.'

Here I said: 'As if you mattered to her.'

She: 'Maybe.'

I said: 'But you don't matter to her or to anybody.'

She: 'I think, you see, I've got to find if there is such a person [for whom I matter], someone to matter to me, someone who will be able to receive, to make contact with what my eyes have seen and my ears have heard. Might be better to give up, I don't see . . . I don't . . .' (Sobbing, on the floor, bent over the cushion on the chair.)

Here she pulled herself together by various means characteristic of her, and knelt up.

'You see, I haven't yet really made contact with you at all today.' I made an affirmative grunt.

I would make the observation that so far the material was of the nature of motor and sensory playing of an unorganized or formless nature (cf. p. 45), out of which the experience of hopelessness and sobbing had arisen.

She went on: 'It's like two other people in another room, meeting for the first time. Polite conversation, sitting up on the high chair.'

(I actually do sit on a high chair in this patient's session.)

'I hate it. I feel sick. But it doesn't matter because it's only me.'

Further examples of my behaviour indicating: it's only she, so it doesn't matter, etc.

> (Pause, with sighing, indicating a sense of hopelessness, and worthlessness.)

Arrival (i.e. *after nearly two hours*)

> Now a clinical change had come about. Now for the first time during this session *the patient seemed to be in the room with me*. This was an extra session I had given her to make up for having had to miss her usual time.

She said, as if this were her first remark to me: 'I'm glad you knew I needed this session.'

The material was now about specific hates, and she started a search for some coloured felt pens she knew I had. Then she took a piece of paper and the black felt pen and made a memorial card to her birthday. She called it her 'Deathday'.

> She was now very much present in the room with me. I omit details of a group of observations of the actual, all of which were redolent with hatred.
>
> (Pause.)
>
> Now she started to look back on the session.

'The trouble is I can't remember what I said to you – or was I talking to myself?'

Interpretative intervention

Here I made an interpretation: 'All sorts of things happen and they wither. This is the myriad deaths you have died. But if someone is there, someone who can give you back what has happened, then the details dealt with in this way become part of you, and do not die.'[2]

She now reached for some milk and asked if she could drink it.[3]

I said: 'Drink it up.'

She said: 'Did I tell you . . .?' (Here she reported positive feeling and activities that were of themselves evidence of her being real and living in the actual world.) 'I feel I've made a sort of contact with these people . . . though something here . . .' (return of sobbing, leaning over the back of a chair). 'Where are you? Why am I alone so? . . . Why don't I matter any more?'

Significant childhood memories came up here, to do with birthday presents and the importance of them, and positive and negative birthday experiences.

> I omit a good deal here because to make it intelligible I would need to give new factual information not needed for this presentation. All this was leading up to a neutral zone, with herself here – but in an activity of indeterminate outcome.

'I don't feel I've . . . I feel I've wasted this session.'

(Pause.)

'I feel as though I came to meet somebody and they didn't come.'

[2] That is, the sense of self comes on the basis of an unintegrated state which, however, by definition, is not observed and remembered by the individual, and which is lost unless observed and mirrored back by someone who is trusted and who justifies the trust and meets the dependence.

[3] In this analysis a kettle and a gas ring, coffee, tea, and a certain kind of biscuit are reliably available.

At this point I found myself making links in view of her forgetting from moment to moment, and her need to have details reflected back, with a time factor at work. I reflected back what she was saying, choosing to speak first in terms of her being born (because of the birthday-deathday) and second in terms of my behaviour, my indicating in so many ways that she didn't matter.

She continued: 'You know, I get a feeling sometimes that I was born . . . [breakdown]. If only it hadn't happened! It comes over me – it's not like the depression.'

I said: 'If you hadn't existed at all, it would have been all right.'

She: 'But what is so awful is existence that's negatived! There was never a time when I thought: a good thing to have been born! It's always that it would have been better if I had not been born – but who knows? Might have – I don't know – it's a point: is there nothing there when someone isn't born, or is there a little soul waiting to pop into a body?'

> Now a change of attitude, indicating the beginning of an
> acceptance of my existence.

'I keep stopping you from talking!'

I said: 'You want me to talk now, but you fear I might say something good.'

She said: 'It was in my mind: "Don't make me wish to BE!"[4] That's a line of a poem by Gerard Manley Hopkins.'

We now talked about poetry, how she makes a great deal of use of poetry that she knows by heart, and how she has lived

---

[4] Actual quotation, from the poem 'Carrion Comfort', would be:
  'Not, I'll not . . .
  . . . most weary, cry I *can no more*. I can;
  Can something, hope, wish day come, not choose not to be.'

from poem to poem (like cigarette to cigarette in chain-smoking), but without the poem's meaning being understood or felt as she now understands and feels this poem. (Her quotations are always apt, and usually she is unaware of the meaning.) I referred here to God as I AM, a useful concept when the individual cannot bear to BE.

She said: 'People use God like an analyst — someone to be there while you're playing.'

I said: 'For whom you matter' — and she said: 'I couldn't say that one, because I couldn't be sure.'

I said: 'Did it spoil things when I said this?' (I feared I had mucked up a very good session.)

But she said: 'No! It's different if you say it, because if I matter to you . . . I want to do things to please you . . . you see this is the hell of having had a religious upbringing. Blast the good girls!'

As a self-observation she said: 'That implies I have a wish not to get well.'

> Here was an example of an interpretation made by the patient that could have been stolen from her if I had made it earlier in the session.

I pointed out that the present-day version of *good* for her is to be *well* — i.e. finish analysis, etc.

Now at last I could bring in the dream — that the girl's paintings were no better — *this negative is now positive*. The statement that the patient is not well is true; not well means not good; that she seemed better was false as her life had been false trying to be good in the sense of fitting into the family moral code.

She said: 'Yes, I'm using my eyes, ears, hands as instruments; I never 100 per cent AM. If I let my hands wander. I might find a me — get into touch with a me . . . but I couldn't. I would need to wander for hours. I couldn't let myself go on.'

We discussed the way in which talking *to oneself* does not reflect back, unless this is a carry-over of such talking having been reflected back by *someone not oneself*.

She said: 'I've been trying to show you *me being alone* [the first two hours of the session]; that's the way I go on when alone, though without words at all, as I don't let myself start talking to myself' (that would be madness).

She went on to talk of her use of a lot of mirrors in her room, involving for the self a search by the mirrors for some person to reflect back. (She had been showing me, though I was there, that no person reflects back.) So now I said: 'It *was yourself that was searching.*'[5]

> I am doubtful about this interpretation, because it smacks of reassurance though not intended that way. I meant that she exists in the searching rather than in finding or being found.

She said: 'I'd like to stop searching and just BE. Yes, looking-for is evidence that there is a self.'

Now at last I could refer back to the incident of being the plane, and then it crashed. As a plane she could BE, but then suicide. She accepted this easily and added: 'But I'd rather be and crash than not ever BE.'

> Somewhere soon after this she was able to go away. The work of the session had been done. It will be observed that in a fifty-minute session no effective work could possibly have been done. We had had three hours to waste and to use.

If I could give the next session, it would be found that we took two hours to reach again to the position we had reached this day (which she had forgotten). Then the patient used an expression

[5] Sometimes she quotes: 'It is Margaret you mourn for' (from Hopkins's poem 'Spring and Fall').

that has value in the summing up of what I am trying to convey. She had asked a question, and I said that the answer to the question could take us to a long and interesting discussion, but it was the *question* that interested me. I said: 'You had the idea to ask that question.'

After this she said the very words that I need in order to express my meaning. She said, slowly, with deep feeling: 'Yes, I see, one could postulate the existence of a ME from the question, as from the searching.'

She had now made the essential interpretation in that the question arose out of what can only be called her creativity, creativity that was a coming together after relaxation, which is the opposite of integration.

Comment

The searching can come only from desultory formless functioning, or perhaps from rudimentary playing, as if in a neutral zone. It is only here, in this unintegrated state of the personality, that that which we describe as creative can appear. This if reflected back, but only if reflected back, becomes part of the organized individual personality, and eventually this in summation makes the individual to be, to be found; and eventually enables himself or herself to postulate the existence of the self.

This gives us our indication for therapeutic procedure – to afford opportunity for formless experience, and for creative impulses, motor and sensory, which are the stuff of playing. And on the basis of playing is built the whole of man's experiential existence. No longer are we either introvert or extrovert. We experience life in the area of transitional phenomena, in the exciting interweave of subjectivity and objective observation, and in an area that is intermediate between the inner reality of the individual and the shared reality of the world that is external to individuals.

5

CREATIVITY AND ITS ORIGINS

THE IDEA OF CREATIVITY

I am hoping that the reader will accept a general reference to creativity, not letting the word get lost in the successful or acclaimed creation but keeping it to the meaning that refers to a colouring of the whole attitude to external reality.

It is creative apperception more than anything else that makes the individual feel that life is worth living. Contrasted with this is a relationship to external reality which is one of compliance, the world and its details being recognized but only as something to be fitted in with or demanding adaptation. Compliance carries with it a sense of futility for the individual and is associated with the idea that nothing matters and that life is not worth living. In a tantalizing way many individuals have experienced just enough of creative living to recognize that for most of their time they are living uncreatively, as if caught up in the creativity of someone else, or of a machine.

This second way of living in the world is recognized as illness in psychiatric terms.[1] In some way or other our theory includes a belief that living creatively is a healthy state, and that compliance is a sick basis for life. There is little doubt that the general attitude of our society and the philosophic atmosphere of the age in which we happen to live contribute to this view, the view that we hold here and that we hold at the present time. We might not have held this view elsewhere and in another age.

These two alternatives of living creatively or uncreatively can be very sharply contrasted. My theory would be much simpler than it is if one or other extreme could be expected to be found in any one case or situation. The problem is made obscure because the degree of objectivity we count on when we talk about external reality in terms of an individual is variable. To some extent objectivity is a relative term because what is objectively perceived is by definition to some extent subjectively conceived of.[2]

While this is the exact area under examination in this book we have to take note that for many individuals external reality remains to some extent a subjective phenomenon. In the extreme case the individual hallucinates either at certain specific moments, or perhaps in a generalized way. There exist all sorts of expressions for this state ('fey', 'not all there', 'feet off the ground', 'unreal') and psychiatrically we refer to such individuals as schizoid. We know that such persons can have value as persons in the community and that they may be happy, but we note that there are certain disadvantages for them and especially for those who live with them. They may see the world subjectively and be easily deluded, or else while being firmly based in

---

[1] I have discussed this issue in detail in my paper 'Classification: Is there a Psychoanalytic Contribution to Psychiatric Classification?' (1959–64), and the interested reader can pursue this theme there.

[2] See *The Edge of Objectivity* (Gillespie, 1960), among many works that deal with the creative element in science.

most areas they accept a delusional system in other areas, or they may be not firmly structured in respect of the psychosomatic partnership so that they are said to have poor coordination. Sometimes a physical disability such as defective sight or hearing plays into this state of affairs making a confused picture in which one cannot clearly distinguish between a hallucinating state and a disability based ultimately on a physical abnormality. In the extreme of this state of affairs the person being described is a patient in a mental hospital, either temporarily or permanently, and is labelled schizophrenic.

It is important for us that we find clinically *no sharp line* between health and the schizoid state or even between health and full-blown schizophrenia. While we recognize the hereditary factor in schizophrenia and while we are willing to see the contributions made in individual cases by physical disorders we look with suspicion on any theory of schizophrenia that divorces the subject from the problems of ordinary living and the universals of individual development in a given environment. We do see the vital importance of the environmental provision especially at the very beginning of the individual's infantile life, and for this reason we make a special study of the facilitating environment in human terms, and in terms of human growth in so far as dependence has meaning (cf. Winnicott, 1963b, 1965).

People may be leading satisfactory lives and may do work that is even of exceptional value and yet may be schizoid or schizophrenic. They may be ill in a psychiatric sense because of a weak reality sense. To balance this one would have to state that there are others who are so firmly anchored in objectively perceived reality that they are ill in the opposite direction of being out of touch with the subjective world and with the creative approach to fact.

To some extent we are helped in these difficult matters by remembering that hallucinations are dream phenomena that have come forward into the waking life and that hallucinating is no more of an illness in itself than the corresponding fact that the day's events and the memories of real happenings are drawn across the barrier into sleep and into dreamformation.[3] In fact, if we look at our descriptions of schizoid persons we find we are using words that we use to describe little children and babies, and there we actually expect to find the phenomena that characterize our schizoid and schizophrenic patients.

The problems outlined in this chapter are examined in this book at the point of their origin, that is in the early stages of individual growth and development. In fact, I am concerned with a study of the exact spot at which a baby is 'schizoid' except that this term is not used because of the baby's immaturity and special state relative to the development of personality and the role of the environment.

Schizoid people are not satisfied with themselves any more than are extroverts who cannot get into touch with dream. These two groups of people come to us for psychotherapy because in the one case they do not want to spend their lives irrevocably out of touch with the facts of life, and in the other case because they feel estranged from dream. They have a sense that something is wrong and that there is a dissociation in their personalities, and they would like to be helped to achieve unit status (Winnicott, 1960b) or a state of time-space integration in which there is one self containing everything instead of dissociated elements that exist in compartments,[4] or are scattered around and left lying about.

In order to look into the theory that analysts use in their work to see where creativeness has a place it is necessary, as I have

---

[3] Though this is inherent in Freud's hypothesis of dream-formation, it is a fact that has often been overlooked (cf. Freud, 1900).
[4] I have discussed a specific instance of this elsewhere (1966), in terms of obsessional neurosis.

already stated, to separate the idea of the creation from works of art. It is true that a creation can be a picture or a house or a garden or a costume or a hairstyle or a symphony or a sculpture; anything from a meal cooked at home. It would perhaps be better to say that these things could be creations. The creativity that concerns me here is a universal. It belongs to being alive. Presumably it belongs to the aliveness of some animals as well as of human beings, but it must be less strikingly significant in terms of animals or of human beings with low intellectual capacity[5] than it is with human beings who have near-average, average, or high intellectual capacity. The creativity that we are studying belongs to the approach of the individual to external reality. Assuming reasonable brain capacity, enough intelligence to enable the individual to become a person living and taking part in the life of the community, everything that happens is creative except in so far as the individual is ill, or is hampered by ongoing environmental factors which stifle his creative processes.

In regard to the second of these two alternatives it is probably wrong to think of creativity as something that can be destroyed utterly. But when one reads of individuals dominated at home, or spending their lives in concentration camps or under lifelong persecution because of a cruel political régime, one first of all feels that it is only a few of the victims who remain creative. These, of course, are the ones that suffer (see Winnicott, 1968b). It appears at first as if all the others who exist (not live) in such pathological communities have so far given up hope that they no longer suffer, and they must have lost the characteristic that makes them human, so that they no longer see the world creatively. These circumstances concern the negative of civilization. This is looking at the destruction of creativity in individuals by

---

[5] A distinction must be made between primary mental defect and clinical defect secondary to schizophrenia of childhood and autism, etc.

environmental factors acting at a late date in personal growth (cf. Bettelheim, 1960).

What is being attempted here is to find a way of studying the loss by individuals of the creative entry into life or of the initial creative approach to external phenomena. I am concerned with aetiology. In the extreme case there is a relative failure *ab initio* in the establishment of a personal capacity for creative living.

As I have already indicated, one has to allow for the possibility that there cannot be a complete destruction of a human individual's capacity for creative living and that, even in the most extreme case of compliance and the establishment of a false personality, hidden away somewhere there exists a secret life that is satisfactory because of its being creative or original to that human being. Its unsatisfactoriness must be measured in terms of its being hidden, its lack of enrichment through living experience (Winnicott, 1968b).

Let us say that in the severe case all that is real and all that matters and all that is personal and original and creative is hidden, and gives no sign of its existence. The individual in such an extreme case would not really mind whether he or she were alive or dead. Suicide is of small importance when such a state of affairs is powerfully organized in an individual, and even the individual himself or herself has no awareness of what might have been or of what has been lost or is missing (Winnicott, 1960a).

The creative impulse is therefore something that can be looked at as a thing in itself, something that of course is necessary if an artist is to produce a work of art, but also as something that is present when *anyone* – baby, child, adolescent, adult, old man or woman – looks in a healthy way at anything or does anything deliberately, such as making a mess with faeces or prolonging the act of crying to enjoy a musical sound. It is present as much in the moment-by-moment living of a backward child who is enjoying breathing as it is in the inspiration of an architect who suddenly knows what it is that he wishes to construct, and who is thinking in terms of material that can actually be used so that his creative impulse may take form and shape, and the world may witness.

Where psychoanalysis has attempted to tackle the subject of creativity it has to a large extent lost sight of the main theme. The analytic writer has perhaps taken some outstanding personality in the creative arts and has tried to make secondary and tertiary observations, ignoring everything that one could call primary. It is possible to take Leonardo da Vinci and make very important and interesting comments on the relationship between his work and certain events that took place in his infancy. A great deal can be done interweaving the themes of his work with his homo-sexual trend. But these and other circumstances in the study of great men and women by-pass the theme that is at the centre of the idea of creativity. It is inevitable that such studies of great men tend to irritate artists and creative people in general. It could be that these studies that we are tempted to make are irritating because they look as if they are getting somewhere, as if they will soon be able to explain why this man was great and that woman achieved much, but the direction of inquiry is wrong. The main theme is being circumvented, that of the creative impulse itself. The creation stands between the observer and the artist's creativity.

It is not of course that anyone will ever be able to explain the creative impulse, and it is unlikely that anyone would ever want to do so; but the link can be made, and usefully made, between creative living and living itself, and the reasons can be studied why it is that creative living can be lost and why the individual's feeling that life is real or meaningful can disappear.

One could suppose that before a certain era, say a thousand years ago, only a very few people lived creatively (cf. Foucault, 1966). To explain this one would have to say that before a certain date it is possible that there was only very exceptionally a man or woman who achieved unit status in personal development. Before a certain date the vast millions of the world of human beings quite possibly never found or certainly soon lost at the end of infancy or childhood their sense of being individuals. This theme is developed a little in Freud's *Moses and Monotheism* (1939) and is referred to in a footnote which I consider to be a very important detail in Freud's writings: 'Breasted calls him "the first individual in human history".' We cannot easily identify ourselves with men and women of early times who so identified themselves with the community and with nature and with unexplained phenomena such as the rising and setting of the sun, thunderbolts and earthquakes. A body of science was needed before men and women could become units integrated in terms of time and space, who could live creatively and exist as individuals. The subject of monotheism belongs to the arrival of this stage in human mental functioning.

A further contribution to the subject of creativity came from Melanie Klein (1957). This contribution results from Klein's recognition of aggressive impulses and destructive fantasy dating from very early in the life of the individual baby. Klein takes up the idea of the destructiveness of the baby and gives it proper emphasis, at the same time making a new and vital issue out of the idea of the fusion of erotic and destructive impulses as a sign of health. The Klein statement includes the concept of reparation and restitution. In my opinion, however, Klein's important work does not reach to the subject of creativity itself and therefore it could easily have the effect of further obscuring the main issue. We do need her work, however, on the central position of the guilt sense. Behind this is Freud's basic concept of ambivalence as an aspect of individual maturity.

Health can be looked at in terms of fusion (erotic and destructive drives) and this makes more urgent than ever the examination of the origin of aggression and of destructive fantasy. For many years in psychoanalytic metapsychology aggression seemed to be explained on the basis of anger.

I have put forward the idea that both Freud and Klein jumped over an obstacle at this point and took refuge in heredity. The concept of the death instinct could be described as a reassertion of the principle of original sin. I have tried to develop the theme that what both Freud and Klein avoided in so doing was the full implication of dependence and therefore of the environmental factor (Winnicott, 1960b). If dependence really does mean dependence, then the history of an individual baby cannot be written in terms of the baby alone. It must be written in terms also of the environmental provision which either meets dependence needs or fails to meet them (Winnicott, 1945, 1948, 1952).

It is hoped that psychoanalysts will be able to use the theory of transitional phenomena in order to describe the way in which good-enough environmental provision at the very earliest stages makes it possible for the individual to cope with the immense shock of loss of omnipotence.[6] What I have called the 'subjective object' (Winnicott, 1962) becomes gradually related to objects that are objectively perceived, but this happens only when a good-enough environmental provision or 'average expectable environment' (Hartmann, 1939) enables the baby to be mad in one particular way that is conceded to babies. This madness only becomes true madness if it appears in later life. At the stage of infancy it is the same subject as that to which I referred when I talked about the acceptance of the paradox, as when a baby creates an object but the object would not have been created as such if it had not already been there.

We find either that individuals live creatively and feel that life is worth living or else that they cannot live creatively and are

---

[6] This antedates the relief that comes from such mental mechanisms as cross-identification.

doubtful about the value of living. This variable in human beings is directly related to the quality and quantity of environmental provision at the beginning or in the early phases of each baby's living experience.

Whereas every effort is made by analysts to describe the psychology of the individual and the dynamic processes of development and defence organization, and to include impulse and drive in terms of the individual, here at this point where creativity either comes into being or does not come into being (or alternatively is lost) the theoretician must take the environment into account, and no statement that concerns the individual as an isolate can touch this central problem of the source of creativity.

It seems important here to refer to a special complication that arises out of the fact that while men and women have much in common they are nevertheless also unalike. Obviously creativity is one of the common denominators, one of the things that men and women share, or they share distress at the loss or absence of creative living. I now propose to examine this subject from another angle.

THE SPLIT-OFF MALE AND FEMALE ELEMENTS TO BE FOUND IN MEN AND WOMEN[7]

There is nothing new either inside or outside psychoanalysis in the idea that men and women have a 'predisposition towards bisexuality'.

I try here to use what I have learned about bisexuality from analyses that have gone step by step towards a certain point and have focused on one detail. No attempt will be made here to trace the steps by which an analysis comes to this kind of

[7] Paper read to the British Psycho-Analytical Society, 2 February 1966, and revised for publication in Forum.

material. It can be said that a great deal of work usually has had to be done before this type of material has become significant and calls for priority. It is difficult to see how all this preliminary work can be avoided. The slowness of the analytic process is a manifestation of a defence the analyst must respect, as we respect all defences. While it is the patient who is all the time teaching the analyst, the analyst should be able to know, theoretically, about the matters that concern the deepest or most central features of personality, else he may fail to recognize and to meet new demands on his understanding and technique when at long last the patient is able to bring deeply buried matters into the content of the transference, thereby affording opportunity for mutative interpretation. The analyst, by interpreting, shows how much and how little of the patient's communication he is able to receive.

As a basis for the idea that I wish to give in this chapter I suggest that creativity is one of the common denominators of men and women. In another language, however, creativity is the prerogative of women, and in yet another language it is a masculine feature. It is this last of the three that concerns me in what follows here.

Clinical data

Illustrative case

I propose to start with a clinical example. This concerns the treatment of a man of middle age, a married man with a family, and successful in one of the professions. The analysis has proceeded along classical lines. This man has had a long analysis and I am not by any means his first psychotherapist. A great deal of work has been done by him and by each of us therapists and analysts in turn, and much change has been brought about in his personality. But there is still something he avers that makes it impossible for him to stop. He knows that what he came for he has not reached. If he cuts his losses the sacrifice is too great.

In the present phase of this analysis something has been reached which is new for me. It has to do with the way I am dealing with the non-masculine element in his personality.

> On a Friday the patient came and reported much as usual. The thing that struck me on this Friday was that the patient was talking about *penis envy*. I use this term advisedly, and I must invite acceptance of the fact that this term was appropriate here in view of the material, and of its presentation. Obviously this term, penis envy, is not usually applied in the description of a man.
>
> The change that belongs to this particular phase is shown in the way I handled this. On this particular occasion I said to him: 'I am listening to a girl. I know perfectly well that you are a man but I am listening to a girl, and I am talking to a girl. I am telling this girl: "You are talking about penis envy." '
>
> I wish to emphasize that this has nothing to do with homosexuality.
>
> (It has been pointed out to me that my interpretation in each of its two parts could be thought of as related to playing, and as far as possible removed from authoritative interpretation that is next door to indoctrination.)
>
> It was clear to me, by the profound effect of this interpretation, that my remark was in some way apposite, and indeed I would not be reporting this incident in this context were it not for the fact that the work that started on this Friday did in fact break into a vicious circle. I had grown accustomed to a routine of good work, good interpretations, good immediate results, and then destruction and disillusionment that followed each time because of the patient's gradual recognition that something fundamental had remained unchanged; there was this unknown factor which had kept this man working at his own

analysis for a quarter of a century. Would his work with me suffer the same fate as his work with the other therapists?

On this occasion there was an immediate effect in the form of intellectual acceptance, and relief, and then there were more remote effects. After a pause the patient said: 'If I were to tell someone about this girl I would be called mad.'

The matter could have been left there, but I am glad, in view of subsequent events, that I went further. It was my next remark that surprised me, and it clinched the matter. I said: 'It was not that *you* told this to anyone; it is *I* who see the girl and hear a girl talking, when actually there is a man on my couch. The mad person is *myself*.'

I did not have to elaborate this point because it went home. The patient said that he now felt sane in a mad environment. In other words he was now released from a dilemma. As he said, subsequently, 'I myself could never say (knowing myself to be a man) "I am a girl". I am not mad that way. But you said it, and you have spoken to both parts of me.'

This madness which was mine enabled him to see himself as a girl *from my position*. He knows himself to be a man, and never doubts that he is a man.

Is it obvious what was happening here? For my part, I have needed to live through a deep personal experience in order to arrive at the understanding I feel I now have reached.

This complex state of affairs has a special reality for this man because he and I have been driven to the conclusion (though unable to prove it) that his mother (who is not alive now) saw a girl baby when she saw him as a baby before she came round to thinking of him as a boy. In other words this man had to fit into her idea that her baby would be and was a girl. (He was the second child, the first being a boy.) We have very good evidence from inside the analysis that in her early management of him the mother held him and dealt with him in all sorts of physical ways as if she failed to see him as a male. On the basis of this pattern he later arranged his defences, but it was the mother's 'madness' that saw a girl where there was a boy, and this was brought right into the present by my having said 'It is I who am mad'. On this Friday he went away profoundly moved and feeling that this was the first significant shift in the analysis for a long time (although, as I have said, there had always been continuous progress in the sense of good work being done).[8]

I would like to give further details relative to this Friday incident. When he came on the following Monday he told me that he was ill. It was quite clear to me that he had an infection and I reminded him that his wife would have it the next day, which in fact happened. Nevertheless, he was inviting me to *interpret* this illness, which started on the Saturday, as if it were psychosomatic. What he tried to tell me was that on the Friday night he had had a satisfactory sexual intercourse with his wife, and so he *ought* to have felt better on the Saturday, but instead of feeling better he had become ill and had felt ill. I was able to leave aside the physical disorder and talk about the incongruity of his feeling ill after the intercourse that he felt ought to have been a healing experience. (He might, indeed, have said: 'I have 'flu, but in spite of that I feel better in myself.')

My interpretation continued along the line started up on the Friday. I said: 'You feel as if you ought to be pleased that here was an interpretation of mine that had released masculine behaviour. *The girl that I was talking to, however, does not want the man released*, and indeed she is not interested in him. What she wants is full acknowledgement of herself and of her own rights over your body. Her penis envy especially includes envy of you as a male.' I went on: 'The feeling ill is a protest from the female self, this girl, because she has always hoped that the analysis would in fact find out that this man, yourself, is and always has

---

[8] For a detailed discussion of the mirror-role of mother in child development see Chapter 9.

been a girl (and "being ill" is a pregenital pregnancy). The only end to the analysis that this girl can look for is the discovery that in fact you are a girl.' Out of this one could begin to understand his conviction that the analysis could never end.[9]

In the subsequent weeks there was a great deal of material confirming the validity of my interpretation and my attitude, and the patient felt that he could see now that his analysis had ceased to be under doom of interminability.

Later I was able to see that the patient's resistance had now shifted to a denial of the importance of my having said 'It is I who am mad'. He tried to pass this off as just my way of putting things – a figure of speech that could be forgotten. I found, however, that here is one of those examples of delusional transference that puzzle patients and analysts alike, and the crux of the problem of management is just here in this interpretation, which I confess I nearly did not allow myself to make.

When I gave myself time to think over what had happened I was puzzled. Here was no new theoretical concept, here was no new principle of technique. In fact, I and my patient had been over this ground before. Yet we had here something new, new in my own attitude and new in his capacity to make use of my interpretative work. I decided to surrender myself to whatever this might mean in myself, and the result is to be found in this paper that I am presenting.

Dissociation

The first thing I noticed was that I had never before fully accepted the complete dissociation between the man (or

---

[9] It will be understood, I hope, that I am not suggesting that this man's very real physical illness, 'flu, was brought about by the emotional trends that coexisted with the physical.

woman) and the aspect of the personality that has the opposite sex. In the case of this man patient the dissociation was nearly complete.

Here, then, I found myself with a new edge to an old weapon, and I wondered how this would or could affect the work I was doing with other patients, both men and women, or boys and girls. I decided, therefore, to study this type of dissociation, leaving aside but not forgetting all the other types of splitting.

Male and female elements in men and women[10]

There was in this case a dissociation that was on the point of breaking down. The dissociation defence was giving way to an acceptance of bisexuality as a quality of the unit or total self. I saw that I was dealing with what could be called a *pure female element*. At first it surprised me that I could reach this only by looking at the material presented by a male patient.[11]

---

[10] I shall continue to use this terminology (male and female elements) for the time being, since I know of no other suitable descriptive terms. Certainly 'active' and 'passive' are not correct terms, and I must continue the argument using the terms that are available.

[11] It would be logical here to follow up the work this man and I did together with a similar piece of work involving a girl or a woman patient. For instance, a young woman reminds me of old material belonging to her early latency when she longed to be a boy. She spent much time and energy willing herself a penis. She needed, however, a special piece of understanding, which was that she, an obvious girl, happy to be a girl, at the same time (with a 10 per cent dissociated part) knew and always had known that she was a boy. Associated with this was a certainty of having been castrated and so deprived of destructive potential, and along with this was murder of mother and the whole of her masochistic defence organization which was central in her personality structure.

Giving clinical examples here involves me in a risk of distracting the reader's attention from my main theme; also, if my ideas are true and universal, then each reader will have personal cases illustrating the place of dissociation rather than of repression related to male and female elements in men and women.

A further clinical observation belongs to this case. Some of the relief that followed our arrival at the new platform for our work together came from the fact that we now could explain why my interpretations, made on good grounds, in respect of use of objects, oral erotic satisfactions in the transference, oral sadistic ideas in respect of the patient's interest in the analyst as part-object or as a person with breast or penis – why such interpretations were never mutative. They were accepted, but: so what? Now that the new position had been reached the patient felt a sense of relationship with me, and this was extremely vivid. It had to do with identity. The pure female split-off element found a primary unity with me as analyst, and this gave the man a feeling of having started to live. I have been affected by this detail, as will appear in my application to theory of what I have found in this case.

Addendum to the clinical section

It is rewarding to review one's current clinical material keeping in mind this one example of dissociation, the split-off girl element in a male patient. The subject can quickly become vast and complex, so that a few observations must be chosen for special mention.

(a) One may, to one's surprise, find that one is dealing with and attempting to analyse the split-off part, while the main functioning person appears only in projected form. This is like treating a child only to find that one is treating one or other parent by proxy. Every possible variation on this theme may come one's way.

(b) The other-sex element may be completely split off so that, for instance, a man may not be able to make any link at all with the split-off part. This applies especially when the personality is otherwise sane and integrated. Where the functioning personality is already organized into multiple splits there is less accent on 'I am sane', and therefore less resistance against the idea 'I am a girl' (in the case of a man) or 'I am a boy' (in the case of a girl).

(c) There may be found clinically a near-complete other-sex dissociation, organized in relation to external factors at a very early date, mixed in with later dissociations organized as a defence, based more or less on cross-identifications. The reality of this later organized defence may militate against the patient's revival in the analysis of the earlier reactive split.

(There is an axiom here, that a patient will always cling to the full exploitation of personal and internal factors, which give him or her a measure of omnipotent control, rather than allow the idea of a crude reaction to an environmental factor, whether distortion or failure. Environmental influence, bad or even good, comes into our work as a traumatic idea, intolerable because not operating within the area of the patient's omnipotence. Compare the melancholic's claim to be responsible for all evil.)

(d) The split-off other-sex part of the personality tends to remain of one age, or to grow but slowly. As compared with this, the truly imaginative figures of the person's inner psychic reality mature, interrelate, grow old, and die. For instance, a man who depends on younger girls for keeping his split-off girl-self alive may gradually become able to employ for his special purpose girls of marriageable age. But should he live to ninety it is unlikely that the girls so employed will reach thirty. Yet in a man patient the girl (hiding the pure girl element of earlier formation) may have girl characteristics, may be breast-proud, experience penis envy, become pregnant, be equipped with no male external genitalia and even possess female sexual equipment and enjoy female sexual experience.

(e) An important issue here is the assessment of all this in terms of psychiatric health. The man who initiates girls into sexual experience may well be one who is more identified with the girl than with himself. This gives him the capacity to go all out to wake up the girl's sex and to satisfy her. He pays for this by getting but little male satisfaction himself, and he pays also in terms of his need to seek always a new girl, this being the opposite of object-constancy.

At the other extreme is the illness of impotence. In between the two lies the whole range of relative potency mixed with dependence of various types and degrees. What is normal depends on the social expectation of any one social group at any one particular time. Could it not be said that at the patriarchal extreme of society sexual inter-course is rape, and at the matriarchal extreme the man with a split-off female element who must satisfy many women is at a premium even if in doing so he annihilates himself?

In between the extremes is bisexuality and an expectation of sexual experience which is less than optimal. This goes along with the idea that social health is mildly depressive – except for holidays.

It is interesting that the existence of this split-off female element actually prevents homosexual practice. In the case of my patient he always fled from homosexual advances at the critical moment because (as he came to see and to tell me) putting homosexuality into practice would establish his maleness which (from the split-off female element self) he never wanted to know for certain.

(In the normal, where bisexuality is a fact, homosexual ideas do not conflict in this way largely because the anal factor (which is a secondary matter) has not attained supremacy over fellatio, and in the fantasy of a fellatio union the matter of the person's biological sex is not significant.)

(f) It seems that in the evolution of Greek myth the first homosexuals were men who imitated women so as to get into as close as possible a relationship with the supreme goddess. This belonged to a matriarchal era out of which a patriarchal god system appeared with Zeus as head. Zeus (symbol of the patriarchal system) initiated the idea of the boy loved sexually by man, and along with this went the relegation of women to a lower status. If this is a true statement of the history of the development of ideas, it gives the link that I need if I am to be able to join my clinical observations about the split-off female element in the case of men patients with the theory of object-relating. (The split-off male element in women patients is of equal importance in our work, but what I have to say about object-relating can be said in terms of one only of the two possible examples of dissociation.)

Summary of preliminary observations

In our theory it is necessary to allow for both a male and a female element in boys and men and girls and women. These elements may be split off from each other to a high degree. This idea requires of us both a study of the clinical effects of this type of dissociation and an examination of the distilled male and female elements themselves.

I have made some observations on the first of these two, the clinical effects; now I wish to examine what I am calling the distilled male and female elements (not male and female persons).

Pure male and pure female elements

Speculation about contrast in kinds of object-relating

Let us compare and contrast the unalloyed male and female elements in the context of object-relating.

I wish to say that the element that I am calling 'male' does traffic in terms of active relating or passive being related to, each being backed by instinct. It is in the development of this idea that we speak of instinct drive in the baby's relation to the breast and to feeding, and subsequently in relation to all the experiences involving the main erotogenic zones, and to subsidiary drives and satisfactions. My suggestion is that, by contrast, the pure female element relates to the breast (or to the mother) in the sense of *the baby becoming the breast (or mother), in the sense that the object is the subject.* I can see no instinct drive in this.

(There is also to be remembered the use of the word 'instinct' that comes from ethology; however, I doubt very much whether imprinting is a matter that affects the newborn human infant at all. I will say here and now that I believe the whole subject of imprinting is irrelevant to the study of the early object-relating of human infants. It certainly has nothing to do with the trauma of separation at two years, the very place where its prime importance has been assumed.)

The term subjective object has been used in describing the first object, the object *not yet repudiated as a not-me phenomenon*. Here in this relatedness of pure female element to 'breast' is a practical application of the idea of the subjective object, and the experience of this paves the way for the objective subject – that is, the idea of a self, and the feeling of real that springs from the sense of having an identity.

However complex the psychology of the sense of self and of the establishment of an identity eventually becomes as a baby grows, no sense of self emerges except on the basis of this relating in the sense of BEING. This sense of being is something that antedates the idea of being-at-one-with, because there has not yet been anything else except identity. Two separate persons can *feel* at one, but here at the place that I am examining the baby and the object *are* one. The term 'primary identification' has perhaps been used for just this that I am describing and I am trying to show how vitally important this first experience is for the initiation of all subsequent experiences of identification.

Projective and introjective identifications both stem from this place where each is the same as the other.

In the growth of the human baby, as the ego begins to organize, this that I am calling the object-relating of the pure female element establishes what is perhaps the simplest of all experiences, the experience of *being*. Here one finds a true continuity of generations, being which is passed on from one generation to another, via the female element of men and women and of male and female infants. I think this has been said before, but always in terms of women and girls, which confuses the issue. It is a matter of the female elements in both males and females.

By contrast, the object-relating of the male element to the object presupposes separateness. As soon as there is the ego organization available, the baby allows the object the quality of being not-me or separate, and experiences id satisfactions that include anger relative to frustration. Drive satisfaction enhances the separation of the object from the baby, and leads to objectification of the object. Henceforth, on the male element side, identification needs to be based on complex mental mechanisms, mental mechanisms that must be given time to appear, to develop, and to become established as part of the new baby's equipment. On the female element side, however, identity requires so little mental structure that this primary identity can be a feature from very early, and the foundation for simple being can be laid (let us say) from the birth date, or before, or soon after, or from whenever the mind has become free from the handicaps to its functioning due to immaturity and to brain damage associated with the birth process.

Psychoanalysts have perhaps given special attention to this male element or drive aspect of object-relating, and yet have neglected the subject-object identity to which I am drawing attention here, which is at the basis of the capacity to be. The male element *does* while the female element (in males and females) *is*. Here would come in those males in Greek myth who tried to be at one with the supreme goddess. Here also is a way of stating a male person's very deep-seated envy of women whose female element men take for granted, sometimes in error.

It seems that frustration belongs to satisfaction-seeking. To the experience of being belongs something else, not frustration, but maiming. I wish to study this specific detail.

Identity: child and breast

It is not possible to state what I am calling here the female element's relation to the breast without the concept of the good-enough and the not-good-enough mother.

(Such an observation is even more true in this area than it is in the comparable area covered by the terms transitional phenomena and transitional objects. The transitional object represents the mother's ability to present the world in such a way that the infant does not at first have to know that the object is not created by the infant. In our immediate context we may allow a total significance to the meaning of adaptation, the mother either giving the infant the opportunity to feel that the breast is the infant, or else not doing so. The breast here is a symbol not of doing but of being.)

This being a good-enough purveyor of female element must be a matter of very subtle details of handling, and in giving consideration to these matters one can draw on the writing of Margaret Mead and of Erik Erikson, who are able to describe the ways in which maternal care in various types of culture determines at a very early age the patterns of the defences of the individual, and also gives the blueprints for later sublimation. These are very subtle matters that we study in respect of this mother and this child.

The nature of the environmental factor

I now return to the consideration of the very early stage in which the pattern is being laid down by the manner in which the mother in subtle ways handles her infant. I must refer in detail to this very special example of the environmental factor. Either the mother has a breast that is, so that the baby can also be when the baby and mother are not yet separated out in the infant's rudimentary mind; or else the mother is incapable of making this contribution, in which case the baby has to develop without the capacity to be, or with a crippled capacity to be.

(Clinically one needs to deal with the case of the baby who has to make do with an identity with a breast that is active, which is a male element breast, but which is not satisfactory for the initial identity which needs a breast that is, not a breast that does. Instead of 'being like' this baby has to 'do like', or to be done to, which from our point of view here is the same thing.)

The mother who is able to do this very subtle thing that I am referring to does not produce a child whose 'pure female' self is envious of the breast, since for this child the breast is the self and the self is the breast. Envy is a term that might become applicable in the experience of a tantalizing failure of the breast as something that is.

The male and female elements contrasted

These considerations have involved me then in a curious statement about the pure male and the pure female aspects of the infant boy or girl. I have arrived at a position in which I say that object-relating in terms of *this pure female element has nothing to do with drive (or instinct)*. Object-relating backed by instinct drive belongs to the male element in the personality uncontaminated by the female element. This line of argument involves me in great difficulties, and yet it seems as if in a statement of the initial stages of the emotional development of the individual it is necessary to separate out (not boys from girls but) the uncontaminated boy element from the uncontaminated girl element. The classical statement in regard to finding, using, oral erotism, oral sadism, anal stages, etc., arises out of a consideration of the life of the pure male element. Studies of identification based on introjection or on incorporation are studies of the experience of the already mixed male and female elements. Study of the pure female element leads us elsewhere.

The study of the pure distilled uncontaminated female element leads us to BEING, and this forms the only basis for self-discovery and a sense of existing (and then on to the capacity to develop an inside, to be a container, to have a capacity to use the mechanisms of projection and introjection and to relate to the world in terms of introjection and projection).

At risk of being repetitious I wish to restate: when the girl element in the boy or girl baby or patient finds the breast it is the self that has been found. If the question is asked, what does the girl baby do with the breast? – the answer must be that this girl element *is* the breast and shares the qualities of breast and mother and is desirable. In the course of time, desirable means edible and this means that the infant is in danger because of being desirable, or, in more sophisticated language, exciting. Exciting implies: liable to make someone's male element *do* something. In this way a man's penis may be an exciting female element generating male element activity in the girl. But (it must be made clear) no girl or woman is like this; in health, there is a variable amount of girl element in a girl, and in a boy. Also, hereditary factor elements enter in, so that it would easily be possible to find a boy with a stronger girl element than the girl standing next to him, who may have less pure female element potential. Add to this the variable capacity of mothers to hand on the desirability of the good breast or of that part of the maternal function that the good breast symbolizes, and it can be seen that some boys and girls are doomed to grow up with a lop-sided bisexuality, loaded on the wrong side of their biological provision.

I am reminded of the question: what is the nature of the communication Shakespeare offers in his delineation of Hamlet's personality and character?

Hamlet is mainly about the awful dilemma that Hamlet found himself in, and there was no solution for him because of the dissociation that was taking place in him as a defence mechanism. It would be rewarding to hear an actor play Hamlet with this in mind. This actor would have a special way of delivering the first line of the famous soliloquy: 'To be, or not to be . . .' He would say, as if trying to get to the bottom of something that cannot be fathomed, 'To be, . . . or . . .' and then he would pause, because in fact the character Hamlet does not know the alternative. At last he would come in with the rather banal alternative: '. . . or not to be'; and then he would be well away on a journey that can lead nowhere. 'Whether 'tis nobler in the mind to suffer / The slings and arrows of outrageous fortune, / Or to take arms against a sea of troubles, / And by opposing end them?' (Act III, Sc. 1). Here Hamlet has gone over into the sado-masochistic alternative, and he has left aside the theme he started with. The rest of the play is a long working-out of the statement of the problem. I mean: Hamlet is depicted at this stage as searching for an alternative to the idea 'To be'. He was searching for a way to state the dissociation that had taken place in his personality between his male and female elements, elements which had up to the time of the death of his father lived together in harmony, being but aspects of his richly endowed person. Yes, inevitably I write as if writing of a person, not a stage character.

As I see it, this difficult soliloquy is difficult because Hamlet had himself not got the clue to his dilemma – since it lay in his own changed state. Shakespeare had the clue, but Hamlet could not go to Shakespeare's play.

If the play is looked at in this way it seems possible to use Hamlet's altered attitude to Ophelia and his cruelty to her as a picture of his ruthless rejection of his own female element, now split off and handed over to her, with his unwelcome male element threatening to take over his whole personality. The cruelty to Ophelia can be a measure of his reluctance to abandon his split-off female element.

In this way it is the play (if Hamlet could have read it, or seen it acted) that could have shown him the nature of his dilemma. The play within the play failed to do this, and I would say that it was staged by him to bring to life his male element which was challenged to the full by the tragedy that had become interwoven with it.

It could be found that the same dilemma in Shakespeare himself provides the problem behind the content of the sonnets. But this is to ignore or even insult the main feature of the sonnets, namely, the poetry. Indeed, as Professor L. C. Knights (1946) specifically insists, it is only too easy to forget the poetry of the plays in writing of the dramatis personae as if they were historical persons.

Summary

1. I have examined the implications for me in my work of my new degree of recognition of the importance of dissociation in some men and women in respect of these male or female elements and the parts of their personalities that are built on these foundations.

2. I have looked at the artificially dissected male and female elements, and I have found that, for the time being, I associate impulse related to objects (also the passive voice of this) with the male element, whereas I find that the characteristic of the female element in the context of object-relating is identity, giving the child the basis for being, and then, later on, a basis for a sense of self. But I find that it is here, in the absolute dependence on maternal provision of that special quality by which the mother meets or fails to meet the earliest functioning of the female element, that we may seek the foundation for the experience of being. I wrote: 'There is thus no sense in making use of the word "id" for phenomena that are not covered and catalogued and experienced and eventually interpreted by ego functioning' (Winnicott, 1962).

Now I want to say: 'After being – doing and being done to. But first, being.'

Added note on the subject of stealing

Stealing belongs to the male element in boys and girls. The question arises: what corresponds to this in terms of the female element in boys and girls? The answer can be that in respect of this element the individual usurps the mother's position and her seat or garments, in this way deriving desirability and seductiveness stolen from the mother.

6

THE USE OF AN OBJECT AND RELATING THROUGH IDENTIFICATIONS[1]

In this chapter I propose to put forward for discussion the idea of the use of an object. The allied subject of relating to objects seems to me to have had our full attention. The idea of the use of an object has not, however, been so much examined, and it may not even have been specifically studied.

This work on the use of an object arises out of my clinical experience and is in the direct line of development that is peculiarly mine. I cannot assume, of course, that the way in which my ideas have developed has been followed by others, but I should like to point out that there has been a sequence, and the order that there may be in the sequence belongs to the evolution of my work.

[1] Based on a paper read to the New York Psychoanalytic Society, 12 November 1968, and published in the *International Journal of Psycho-Analysis*, Vol. 50 (1969).

What I have to say in this present chapter is extremely simple. Although it comes out of my psychoanalytical experience I would not say that it could have come out of my psychoanalytical experience of two decades ago, because I would not then have had the technique to make possible the transference movements that I wish to describe. For instance, it is only in recent years that I have become able to wait and wait for the natural evolution of the transference arising out of the patient's growing trust in the psychoanalytic technique and setting, and to avoid breaking up this natural process by making interpretations. It will be noticed that I am talking about the making of interpretations and not about interpretations as such. It appals me to think how much deep change I have prevented or delayed in patients in *a certain classification category* by my personal need to interpret. If only we can wait, the patient arrives at understanding creatively and with immense joy, and I now enjoy this joy more than I used to enjoy the sense of having been clever. I think I interpret mainly to let the patient know the limits of my understanding. The principle is that it is the patient and only the patient who has the answers. We may or may not enable him or her to encompass what is known or become aware of it with acceptance.

By contrast with this comes the interpretative work that the analyst must do, which distinguishes analysis from self-analysis. This interpreting by the analyst, if it is to have effect, must be related to the patient's ability *to place the analyst outside the area of subjective phenomena*. What is then involved is the patient's ability to use the analyst, which is the subject of this paper. In teaching, as in the feeding of a child, the capacity to use objects is taken for granted, but in our work it is necessary for us to be concerned with the development and establishment of the capacity to use objects and to recognize a patient's inability to use objects, where this is a fact.

It is in the analysis of the borderline type of case that one has

the chance to observe the delicate phenomena that give point-
ers to an understanding of truly schizophrenic states. By the
term 'a borderline case' I mean the kind of case in which the
core of the patient's disturbance is psychotic, but the patient
has enough psychoneurotic organization always to be able to
present psychoneurosis or psychosomatic disorder when the
central psychotic anxiety threatens to break through in crude
form. In such cases the psychoanalyst may collude for years
with the patient's need to be psychoneurotic (as opposed to
mad) and to be treated as psychoneurotic. The analysis goes
well, and everyone is pleased. The only drawback is that the
analysis never ends. It can be terminated, and the patient may
even mobilize a psychoneurotic false self for the purpose of
finishing and expressing gratitude. But, in fact, the patient
knows that there has been no change in the underlying (psychotic) state and that the analyst and the patient have succeeded in
colluding to bring about a failure. Even this failure may have
value if both analyst and patient acknowledge the failure. The
patient is older and the opportunities for death by accident or
disease have increased, so that actual suicide may be avoided.
Moreover, it has been fun while it lasted. If psychoanalysis
could be a way of life, then such a treatment might be said to
have done what it was supposed to do. But psychoanalysis is no
way of life. We all hope that our patients will finish with us and
forget us, and that they will find living itself to be the therapy
that makes sense. Although we write papers about these borderline cases we are inwardly troubled when the madness that is
there remains undiscovered and unmet. I have tried to state
this in a broader way in a paper on classification (Winnicott,
1959–64).

It is perhaps necessary to prevaricate a little longer to give my
own view on the difference between object-relating and object-
usage. In object-relating the subject allows certain alterations in
the self to take place, of a kind that has caused us to invent the

term 'cathexis'. The object has become meaningful. Projection mechanisms and identifications have been operating, and the subject is depleted to the extent that something of the subject is found in the object, though enriched by feeling. Accompanying these changes is some degree of physical involvement (however slight) towards excitement, in the direction of the functional climax of an orgasm. (In this context I deliberately omit reference to the aspect of relating that is an exercise in cross-identifications, see p. 175. This must be omitted here because it belongs to a phase of development that is subsequent to and not prior to the phase of development with which I am concerned in this paper, that is to say, the move away from self-containment and relating to subjective objects into the realm of object-usage.)

Object-relating is an experience of the subject that can be described in terms of the subject as an isolate (Winnicott, 1958b, 1963a). When I speak of the use of an object, however, I take object-relating for granted, and add new features that involve the nature and the behaviour of the object. For instance, the object, if it is to be used, must necessarily be real in the sense of being part of shared reality, not a bundle of projections. It is this, I think, that makes for the world of difference that there is between relating and usage.

If I am right in this, then it follows that discussion of the subject of relating is a much easier exercise for analysts than is the discussion of usage, since relating may be examined as a phenomenon of the subject, and psychoanalysis always likes to be able to eliminate all factors that are environmental, except in so far as the environment can be thought of in terms of projective mechanisms. But in examining usage there is no escape: the analyst must take into account the nature of the object, not as a projection, but as a thing in itself.

For the time being may I leave it at that, that relating can be described in terms of the individual subject, and that usage cannot be described except in terms of acceptance of the object's independent existence, its property of having been there all the time. You will see that it is just these problems that concern us when we look at the area that I have tried to draw attention to in my work on what I have called transitional phenomena.

But this change does not come about automatically, by maturational process alone. It is this detail that I am concerned with.

In clinical terms: two babies are feeding at the breast. One is feeding on the self, since the breast and the baby have not yet become (for the baby) separate phenomena. The other is feeding from an other-than-me source, or an object that can be given cavalier treatment without effect on the baby unless it retaliates. Mothers, like analysts, can be good or not good enough; some can and some cannot carry the baby over from relating to usage.

I should like to put in a reminder here that the essential feature in the concept of transitional objects and phenomena (according to my presentation of the subject) is *the paradox, and the acceptance of the paradox*: the baby creates the object, but the object was there waiting to be created and to become a cathected object. I tried to draw attention to this aspect of transitional phenomena by claiming that in the rules of the game we all know that we will never challenge the baby to elicit an answer to the question: did you create that or did you find it?

I am now ready to go straight to the statement of my thesis. It seems I am afraid to get there, as if I fear that once the thesis is stated the purpose of my communication is at an end, because it is so very simple.

To use an object the subject must have developed a *capacity* to use objects. This is part of the change to the reality principle.

This capacity cannot be said to be inborn, nor can its development in an individual be taken for granted. The development of a capacity to use an object is another example of the maturational process as something that depends on a facilitating environment.[2]

In the sequence one can say that first there is object-relating, then in the end there is object-use; in between, however, is the most difficult thing, perhaps, in human development; or the most irksome of all the early failures that come for mending. This thing that there is in between relating and use is the subject's placing of the object outside the area of the subject's omnipotent control; that is, the subject's perception of the object as an external phenomenon, not as a projective entity, in fact recognition of it as an entity in its own right.[3]

This change (from relating to usage) means that the subject destroys the object. From here it could be argued by an armchair philosopher that there is therefore no such thing in practice as the use of an object: if the object is external, then the object is destroyed by the subject. Should the philosopher come out of his chair and sit on the floor with his patient, however, he will find that there is an intermediate position. In other words, he will find that after 'subject relates to object' comes 'subject destroys object' (as it becomes external); and then may come 'object survives destruction by the subject'. But there may or may not be survival. A new feature thus arrives in the theory of object-relating. The subject says to the object: 'I destroyed you', and the object is there to receive the communication. From now on the subject says: 'Hullo object!' 'I destroyed you.' 'I love you.' 'You have value for me because of your survival of my destruction of you.' 'While I am loving you I am all the time destroying you in

---

[2] In choosing *The Maturational Processes and the Facilitating Environment* as the title of my book in the International Psycho-Analytical Library (1965), I was showing how much I was influenced by Dr Phyllis Greenacre (1960) at the Edinburgh Congress. Unfortunately, I failed to put into the book an acknowledgement of this fact.

[3] I was influenced in my understanding of this point by W. Clifford M. Scott (personal communication, *c.* 1940).

(unconscious) *fantasy.*' Here fantasy begins for the individual. The subject can now *use* the object that has survived. It is important to note that it is not only that the subject destroys the object because the object is placed outside the area of omnipotent control. It is equally significant to state this the other way round and to say that it is the destruction of the object that places the object outside the area of the subject's omnipotent control. In these ways the object develops its own autonomy and life, and (if it survives) contributes-in to the subject, according to its own properties.

In other words, because of the survival of the object, the subject may now have started to live a life in the world of objects, and so the subject stands to gain immeasurably; but the price has to be paid in acceptance of the ongoing destruction in unconscious fantasy relative to object-relating.

Let me repeat. This is a position that can be arrived at by the individual in early stages of emotional growth only through the actual survival of cathected objects that are at the time in process of becoming destroyed because real, becoming real because destroyed (being destructible and expendable).

From now on, this stage having been reached, projective mechanisms assist in the act of *noticing what is there*, but they are not *the reason why the object is there*. In my opinion this is a departure from theory which tends to a conception of external reality only in terms of the individual's projective mechanisms.

I have now nearly made my whole statement. Not quite, however, because it is not possible for me to take for granted an acceptance of the fact that the first impulse in the subject's relation to the object (objectively perceived, not subjective) is destructive. (Earlier I used the word 'cavalier', in an attempt to give the reader a chance to imagine something at that point without too clearly pointing the way.)

The central postulate in this thesis is that, whereas the subject does not destroy the subjective object (projection material), destruction turns up and becomes a central feature so far as the object is objectively perceived, has autonomy, and belongs to 'shared' reality. This is the difficult part of my thesis, at least for me.

It is generally understood that the reality principle involves the individual in anger and reactive destruction, but my thesis is that the destruction plays its part in making the reality, placing the object outside the self. For this to happen, favourable conditions are necessary.

This is simply a matter of examining the reality principle under high power. As I see it, we are familiar with the change whereby projection mechanisms enable the subject to take cognizance of the object. This is not the same as claiming that the object exists for the subject because of the operation of the subject's projection mechanisms. At first the observer uses words that seem to apply to both ideas at one and the same time, but under scrutiny we see that the two ideas are by no means identical. It is exactly here that we direct our study.

At the point of development that is under survey the subject is creating the object in the sense of finding externality itself, and it has to be added that this experience depends on the object's capacity to survive. (It is important that 'survive', in this context, means 'not retaliate'.) If it is in an analysis that these matters are taking place, then the analyst, the analytic technique, and the analytic setting all come in as surviving or not surviving the patient's destructive attacks. This destructive activity is the patient's attempt to place the analyst outside the area of omnipotent control, that is, out in the world. Without the experience of maximum destructiveness (object not protected) the subject never places the analyst outside and therefore can never do more than experience a kind of self-analysis, using the analyst as a projection of a part of the self. In terms of feeding, the patient, then, can feed only on the self and cannot use the breast for getting fat. The patient may even enjoy the analytic experience but will not fundamentally change.

And if the analyst is a subjective phenomenon, what about waste disposal? A further statement is needed in terms of output.[4]

In psychoanalytic practice the positive changes that come about in this area can be profound. They do not depend on interpretative work. They depend on the analyst's survival of the attacks, which involves and includes the idea of the absence of a quality change to retaliation. These attacks may be very difficult for the analyst to stand,[5] especially when they are expressed in terms of delusion, or through manipulation which makes the analyst actually do things that are technically bad. (I refer to such a thing as being unreliable at moments when reliability is all that matters, as well as to survival in terms of keeping alive and of absence of the quality of retaliation.)

The analyst feels like interpreting, but this can spoil the process, and for the patient can seem like a kind of self-defence, the analyst parrying the patient's attack. Better to wait till after the phase is over, and then discuss with the patient what has been happening. This is surely legitimate, for as analyst one has one's own needs; but verbal interpretation at this point is not the essential feature and brings its own dangers. The essential feature is the analyst's survival and the intactness of the psycho-analytic technique. Imagine how traumatic can be the actual death of the analyst when this kind of work is in process, although even the actual death of the analyst is not as bad as the development in the analyst of a change of attitude towards retaliation. These are risks that simply must be taken by the

---

[4] The next task for a worker in the field of transitional phenomena is to restate the problem in terms of disposal.

[5] When the analyst knows that the patient carries a revolver, then, it seems to me, this work cannot be done.

patient. Usually the analyst lives through these phases of movement in the transference, and after each phase there comes reward in terms of love, reinforced by the fact of the backcloth of unconscious destruction.

It appears to me that the idea of a developmental phase essentially involving survival of object does affect the theory of the roots of aggression. It is no good saying that a baby of a few days old envies the breast. It is legitimate, however, to say that at whatever age a baby begins to allow the breast an external position (outside the area of projection), then this means that destruction of the breast has become a feature. I mean the actual impulse to destroy. It is an important part of what a mother does, to be the first person to take the baby through this first version of the many that will be encountered, of attack that is survived. This is the right moment in the child's development, because of the child's relative feebleness, so that destruction can fairly easily be survived. However, even so it is a tricky matter; it is only too easy for a mother to react moralistically when her baby bites and hurts.[6] But this language involving 'the breast' is jargon. The whole area of development and management is involved, in which adaptation is related to dependence.

It will be seen that, although destruction is the word I am using, this actual destruction belongs to the object's failure to survive. Without this failure, destruction remains potential. The word 'destruction' is needed, not because of the baby's impulse to destroy, but because of the object's liability not to survive, which also means to suffer change in quality, in attitude.

The way of looking at things that belongs to my presentation of this chapter makes possible a new approach to the whole subject of the roots of aggression. For instance, it is not necessary

[6] In fact, the baby's development is immensely complicated if he or she should happen to be born with a tooth, so that the gum's attack on the breast can never be tried out.

to give inborn aggression more than that which is its due in company with everything else that is inborn. Undoubtedly inborn aggression must be variable in a quantitative sense in the same way that everything else that is inherited is variable as between individuals. By contrast, the variations are great that arise out of the differences in the experiences of various new-born babies according to whether they are or are not carried through this very difficult phase. Such variations in the field of experience are indeed immense. Moreover, the babies that have been seen through this phase well are likely to be more aggres-sive *clinically* than the ones who have not been seen through the phase well, and for whom aggression is something that cannot be encompassed, or something that can be retained only in the form of a liability to be an object of attack.

This involves a rewriting of the theory of the roots of aggres-sion since most of that which has already been written by ana-lysts has been formulated without reference to that which is being discussed in this chapter. The assumption is always there, in orthodox theory, that aggression is reactive to the encounter with the reality principle, whereas here it is the destructive drive that creates the quality of externality. This is central in the structure of my argument.

Let me look for a moment at the exact place of this attack and survival in the hierarchy of relationships. More primitive and quite different is annihilation. Annihilation means 'no hope'; cathexis withers up because no result completes the reflex to produce conditioning. On the other hand, attack in anger relative to the encounter with the reality principle is a more sophisti-cated concept, postdating the destruction that I postulate here. *There is no anger* in the destruction of the object to which I am referring, though there could be said to be joy at the object's survival. From this moment, or arising out of this phase, the object is *in fantasy* always being destroyed. This quality of 'always being destroyed' makes the reality of the surviving object felt as such, strengthens the feeling tone, and contributes to object-constancy. The object can now be used.

I wish to conclude with a note on using and usage. By 'use' I do not mean 'exploitation'. As analysts, we know what it is like to be used, which means that we can see the end of the treatment, be it several years away. Many of our patients come with this problem already solved – they can use objects and they can use us and can use analysis, just as they have used their parents and their siblings and their homes. However, there are many patients who need us to be able to give them a capacity to use us. This for them is the analytic task. In meeting the needs of such patients, we shall need to know what I am saying here about our survival of their destructiveness. A backcloth of unconscious destruction of the analyst is set up and we survive it or, alternatively, here is yet another analysis interminable.

Summary

Object-relating can be described in terms of the experience of the subject. Description of object-usage involves consideration of the nature of the object. I am offering for discussion the reasons why, in my opinion, a capacity to use an object is more sophisticated than a capacity to relate to objects; and relating may be to a subjective object, but usage implies that the object is part of external reality.

This sequence can be observed: (1) Subject relates to object. (2) Object is in process of being found instead of placed by the subject in the world. (3) Subject destroys object. (4) Object survives destruction. (5) Subject can use object.

The object is always being destroyed. This destruction becomes the unconscious backcloth for love of a real object; that is, an object outside the area of the subject's omnipotent control.

Study of this problem involves a statement of the positive value of destructiveness. The destructiveness, plus the object's survival of the destruction, places the object outside the area of objects set up by the subject's projective mental mechanisms. In this way a world of shared reality is created which the subject can use and which can feed back other-than-me substance into the subject.

7

THE LOCATION OF
CULTURAL EXPERIENCE[1]

On the seashore of endless worlds, children play.

Tagore

In this chapter I wish to develop the theme that I stated briefly
on the occasion of the Banquet organized by the British Psycho-
Analytical Society to mark the completion of the *Standard Edition* of
Freud's Works (London, 8 October 1966). In my attempt to pay
tribute to James Strachey I said:

'Freud did not have a place in his topography of the mind for
the experience of things cultural. He gave new value to inner
psychic reality, and from this came a new value for things that
are actual and truly external. Freud used the word "sublimation" to point the way to a place where cultural experience is

[1] Published in the *International Journal of Psycho-Analysis*, Vol. 48, Part 3 (1967).

meaningful, but perhaps he did not get so far as to tell us where in the mind cultural experience is.'

Now I want to enlarge this idea and make an attempt at a positive statement which can be critically examined. I shall use my own language.

The quotation from Tagore has always intrigued me. In my adolescence I had no idea what it could mean, but it found a place in me, and its imprint has not faded.

When I first became a Freudian I knew what it meant. The sea and the shore represented endless intercourse between man and woman, and the child emerged from this union to have a brief moment before becoming in turn adult or parent. Then, as a student of unconscious symbolism, I knew (one always knows) that the sea is the mother, and onto the seashore the child is born. Babies come up out of the sea and are spewed out upon the land, like Jonah from the whale. So now the seashore was the mother's body, after the child is born and the mother and the now viable baby are getting to know each other.

Then I began to see that this employs a sophisticated concept of the parent-infant relationship and that there could be an unsophisticated infantile point of view, a different one from that of the mother or the observer, and that this infant's viewpoint could be profitably examined. For a long time my mind remained in a state of not-knowing, this state crystallizing into my formulation of the transitional phenomena. In the interim I played about with the concept of 'mental representations' and with the description of these in terms of objects and phenomena located in the personal psychic reality, felt to be inside; also, I followed the effects of the operation of the mental mechanisms of projection and introjection. I realized, however, that *play is in fact neither a matter of inner psychic reality nor a matter of external reality*.

Now I have come to the subject-matter of this chapter, and to the question: *if play is neither inside nor outside, where is it?* I was near to the idea that I express here in my paper 'The Capacity to be Alone' (1958b), in which I said that, at first, the child is alone only in the presence of someone. In that paper I did not develop the idea of the common ground in this relationship between the child and the someone.

My patients (especially when regressive and dependent in the transference or transference dreams) have taught me how to find an answer to the question: where is play? I wish to condense what I have learned in my psychoanalytic work into a theoretical statement.

I have claimed that when we witness an infant's employment of a transitional object, the first not-me possession, we are witnessing both the child's first use of a symbol and the first experience of play. An essential part of my formulation of transitional phenomena is that we agree never to make the challenge to the baby: did you create this object, or did you find it conveniently lying around? That is to say, an essential feature of transitional phenomena and objects is a quality in our attitude when we observe them.

The object is a symbol of the union of the baby and the mother (or part of the mother). This symbol can be located. It is at the place in space and time where and when the mother is in transition from being (in the baby's mind) merged in with the infant and alternatively being experienced as an object to be perceived rather than conceived of. The use of an object symbolizes the union of two now separate things, baby and mother, *at the point in time and space of the initiation of their state of separateness.* [2]

A complication exists right from the very beginning of any consideration of this idea, in that it is necessary to postulate that if the use of the object by the baby builds up into anything (i.e. is

---

[2] It is necessary to simplify matters by referring to the use of objects, but the title of my original paper was 'Transitional Objects and Transitional Phenomena' (1951).

more than an activity that might be found even in a baby born with no brain), then there must be the beginning of the setting up in the infant's mind or personal psychic reality of an image of the object. But the mental representation in the inner world is kept significant, or the imago in the inner world is kept alive, by the reinforcement given through the availability of the external separated-off and actual mother, along with her technique of child care.

It is perhaps worth while trying to formulate this in a way that gives the time factor due weight. The feeling of the mother's existence lasts x minutes. If the mother is away more than x minutes, then the imago fades, and along with this the baby's capacity to use the symbol of the union ceases. The baby is distressed, but this distress is soon *mended* because the mother returns in $x+y$ minutes. In $x+y$ minutes the baby has not become altered. But in $x+y+z$ minutes the baby has become *traumatized*. In $x+y+z$ minutes the mother's return does not mend the baby's altered state. Trauma implies that the baby has experienced a break in life's continuity, so that primitive defences now become organized to defend against a repetition of 'unthinkable anxiety' or a return of the acute confusional state that belongs to disintegration of nascent ego structure.

We must assume that the vast majority of babies never experience the $x+y+z$ quantity of deprivation. This means that the majority of children do not carry around with them for life the knowledge from experience of having been mad. Madness here simply means a *break-up* of whatever may exist at the time of *a personal continuity of existence*. After 'recovery' from $x+y+z$ deprivation a baby has to start again permanently deprived of the root which could provide *continuity with the personal beginning*. This implies the existence of a memory system and an organization of memories.

By contrast, from the effects of $x+y+z$ degree of deprivation, babies are constantly being *cured* by the mother's localized spoiling that mends the ego structure. This mending of the ego structure re-establishes the baby's capacity to use a symbol of union; the baby then comes once more to allow and even to benefit from separation. *This is the place that I have set out to examine, the separation that is not a separation but a form of union.*[3]

It was at an important point in the phase of development of these ideas in me in the early forties that Marion Milner (in conversation) was able to convey to me the tremendous significance that there can be in the interplay of the edges of two curtains, or of the surface of a jug that is placed in front of another jug (cf. Milner, 1969).

It is to be noted that the phenomena that I am describing have no climax. This distinguishes them from phenomena that have instinctual backing, where the orgiastic element plays an essential part, and where satisfactions are closely linked with climax.

But these phenomena that have reality in the area whose existence I am postulating belong to the *experience* of relating to objects. One can think of the 'electricity' that seems to generate in meaningful or intimate contact, that is a feature, for instance, when two people are in love. These phenomena of the play area have infinite variability, contrasting with the relative stereotypy of phenomena that relate either to personal body functioning or to environmental actuality.

Psychoanalysts who have rightly emphasized the significance of instinctual experience and of reactions to frustration have failed to state with comparable clearness or conviction the tre-

---

[3] Merrell Middlemore (1941) saw the infinite richness in the intertwined techniques of the nursing couple. She was near what I am attempting to state here. Rich material exists for us to observe and enjoy in this field of the bodily relationship that may (though it may not) exist between baby and mother, especially if in making our observations (whether direct or in psychoanalysis) we are not simply thinking in terms of oral erotism with satisfaction or frustration, etc.

See also Hoffer (1949, 1950).

mendous intensity of these non-climactic experiences that are called playing. Starting as we do from psychoneurotic illness and with ego defences related to anxiety that arises out of the instinctual life, we tend to think of health in terms of the state of ego defences. We say it is healthy when these defences are not rigid, etc. But we seldom reach the point at which we can start to describe what life is like apart from illness or absence of illness.

That is to say, we have yet to tackle the question of *what life itself is about*. Our psychotic patients force us to give attention to this sort of basic problem. We now see that it is not instinctual satisfaction that makes a baby begin to be, to feel that life is real, to find life worth living. In fact, instinctual gratifications start off as part-functions and they become *seductions* unless based on a well-established capacity in the individual person for total experience, and for experience in the area of transitional phenomena. It is the self that must precede the self's use of instinct; the rider must ride the horse, not be run away with. I could use Buffon's saying: 'Le style est l'homme même.' When one speaks of a man one speaks of him *along with* the summation of his cultural experiences. The whole forms a unit.

I have used the term 'cultural experience' as an extension of the idea of transitional phenomena and of play without being certain that I can define the word 'culture'. The accent indeed is on experience. In using the 'word culture' I am thinking of the inherited tradition. I am thinking of something that is in the common pool of humanity, into which individuals and groups of people may contribute, and from which we may all draw *if we have somewhere to put what we find*.

There is a dependence here on some kind of recording method. No doubt a very great deal was lost of the early civilizations, but in the myths that were a product of oral tradition there could be said to be a cultural pool giving the history of human culture spanning six thousand years. This history through myth persists to the present time in spite of the efforts of historians to be objective, which they can never be, though they must try.

Perhaps I have said enough to show both what I know and what I do not know about the meaning of the word 'culture'. It interests me, however, as a side issue, that in any cultural field it is not possible to be original except on a basis of tradition. Conversely, no one in the line of cultural contributors repeats except as a deliberate quotation, and the unforgivable sin in the cultural field is plagiarism. The interplay between originality and the acceptance of tradition as the basis for inventiveness seems to me to be just one more example, and a very exciting one, of the interplay between separateness and union.

I must pursue a little further the topic in terms of the baby's very early experiences, when the various capacities are being initiated, made ontogenetically possible because of the mother's extremely sensitive adaptation to the needs of her baby, based on her identification with the baby. (I refer to the stages of growth before the baby has acquired mental mechanisms that do soon become available for the organizing of complex defences. I repeat here: a human infant must travel some distance from early experiences in order to have the maturity to be deep.)

This theory does not affect what we have come to believe in respect of the aetiology of psychoneurosis, or the treatment of patients who are psychoneurotic; nor does it clash with Freud's structural theory of the mind in terms of ego, id, superego. What I say does affect our view of the question: what is life about? You may cure your patient and not know what it is that makes him or her go on living. It is of first importance for us to acknowledge openly that absence of psychoneurotic illness may be health, but it is not life. Psychotic patients who are all the time hovering between living and not living force us to look at this problem, one that really belongs not to psychoneurotics but to all human beings. I am claiming that these same phenomena that are life and death to our schizoid or borderline patients appear in our cultural experiences. It is these cultural experiences that provide the continuity in the human race that transcends personal existence. I am assuming that cultural experiences are in direct continuity with play, the play of those who have not yet heard of games.

Main thesis

Here, then, is my main statement. I am claiming:

1. The place where cultural experience is located is in the *potential space* between the individual and the environment (originally the object). The same can be said of playing. Cultural experience begins with creative living first manifested in play.
2. For every individual the use of this space is determined by *life experiences* that take place at the early stages of the individual's existence.
3. From the beginning the baby has maximally intense experiences *in the potential space between the subjective object and the object objectively perceived*, between me-extensions and the not-me. This potential space is at the interplay between there being nothing but me and there being objects and phenomena outside omnipotent control.
4. Every baby has his or her own favourable or unfavourable experience here. Dependence is maximal. The potential space happens only *in relation to a feeling of confidence* on the part of the baby, that is, confidence related to the dependability of the mother-figure or environmental elements, confidence being the evidence of dependability that is becoming introjected.
5. In order to study the play and then the cultural life of the individual one must study the fate of the potential space between any one baby and the human (and therefore fallible) mother-figure who is essentially adaptive because of love.

It will be seen that if this area is to be thought of as part of the ego organization, here is a part of the ego that is not a body-ego, that is not founded on the pattern of body functioning but is founded on body experiences. These experiences belong to object-relating of a non-orgiastic kind, or to what can be called ego-relatedness, at the place where it can be said that continuity is giving place to contiguity.

Continuing argument

This statement makes necessary an examination of the fate of this potential space, which may or may not come into prominence as a vital area in the mental life of the developing person.

What happens if the mother is able to start on a graduated failure of adaptation from a position of adapting fully? This is the crux of the matter, and the problem needs study because it affects our technique as analysts when we have patients who are regressed in the sense of being dependent. In the average good experience in this field of management (that starts so early, and that starts and starts again) the baby finds intense, even agonizing, pleasure associated with imaginative play. There is no set game, so everything is creative, and although playing is part of object-relating, whatever happens is personal to the baby. Everything physical is imaginatively elaborated, is invested with a first-time-ever quality. Can I say that this is the meaning intended for the word 'cathect'?

I can see that I am in the territory of Fairbairn's (1941) concept of 'object-seeking' (as opposed to 'satisfaction-seeking').

As observers we note that everything in the play has been done before, has been felt before, has been smelt before, and where there appear specific symbols of the union of baby and mother (transitional objects) these very objects have been adopted, not created. Yet for the baby (if the mother can supply the right conditions) every detail of the baby's life is an example of creative living. Every object is a 'found' object. Given the chance, the baby begins to live creatively, and to use actual objects to be creative into and with. If the baby is not given this chance then there is no area in which the baby may have play, or may have cultural experience; then it follows that there is no link with the cultural inheritance, and there will be no contribution to the cultural pool.

The 'deprived child' is notoriously restless and unable to play, and has an impoverishment of capacity to experience in the cultural field. This observation leads to a study of the effect of deprivation at the time of the loss of what has become accepted as reliable. A study of the effects of loss at any early stage involves us in looking at this intermediate area, or potential space between subject and object. Failure of dependability or loss of object means to the child a loss of the play area, and loss of meaningful symbol. In favourable circumstances the potential space becomes filled with the products of the baby's own creative imagination. In unfavourable circumstances the creative use of objects is missing or relatively uncertain. I have described elsewhere (Winnicott, 1960a) the way in which the defence of the compliant false self appears, with the hiding of the true self that has the potential for creative use of objects.

There is, in cases of premature failure of environmental reliability, an alternative danger, which is that this potential space may become filled with what is injected into it from someone other than the baby. It seems that whatever is in this space that comes from someone else is persecutory material, and the baby has no means of rejecting it. Analysts need to beware lest they create a feeling of confidence and an intermediate area in which play can take place and then inject into this area or inflate it with interpretations which in effect are from their own creative imaginations.

Fred Plaut, a Jungian analyst, has written a paper (1966) from which I quote:

'The capacity to form images and to use these constructively

> by recombination into new patterns is – unlike dreams or
> fantasies – dependent on the individual's ability to trust.'

The word 'trust' in this context shows an understanding of what I mean by the building up of confidence based on experience, at the time of maximal dependence, before the enjoyment and employment of separation and independence.

I suggest that the time has come for psychoanalytic theory to pay tribute to this *third area*, that of cultural experience which is a derivative of play. Psychotics insist on our knowing about it, and it is of great importance in our assessment of the lives rather than the health of human beings. (The other two areas are inner or personal psychic reality and the actual world with the individual living in it.)

Summary

I have tried to draw attention to the importance both in theory and in practice of a third area, that of play, which expands into creative living and into the whole cultural life of man. This third area has been contrasted with inner or personal psychic reality and with the actual world in which the individual lives, which can be objectively perceived. I have located this important area of *experience* in the potential space between the individual and the environment, that which initially both joins and separates the baby and the mother when the mother's love, displayed or made manifest as human reliability, does in fact give the baby a sense of trust or of confidence in the environmental factor.

Attention is drawn to the fact that this potential space is a highly variable factor (from individual to individual), whereas the two other locations – personal or psychic reality and the actual world – are relatively constant, one being biologically determined and the other being common property.

The potential space between baby and mother, between child and family, between individual and society or the world, depends on experience which leads to trust. It can be looked upon as sacred to the individual in that it is here that the individual experiences creative living.

By contrast, exploitation of this area leads to a pathological condition in which the individual is cluttered up with persecutory elements of which he has no means of ridding himself.

It may perhaps be seen from this how important it can be for the analyst to recognize the existence of this place, the only place where play can start, a place that is at the continuity-contiguity moment, where transitional phenomena originate.

My hope is that I have begun to answer my own question: where is cultural experience located?

8

THE PLACE WHERE WE LIVE[1]

I wish to examine the place, using the word in an abstract sense, where we most of the time are when we are experiencing life.

By the language we use we show our natural interest in this matter. I may be in a muddle, and then I either crawl out of the muddle or else try to put things in order so that I may, at least for a time, know *where I am*. Or I may feel I am *at sea*, and I take bearings so that I may come to port (any port in a storm), and then when I am on dry land I look for a house built *on rock* rather than *on sand*; and in my own home, which (as I am English) is my castle, I am in a seventh heaven.

Without straining the language of everyday use I may talk of my behaviour in the world of external (or shared) reality, or I may be having an inner or mystical experience, while squatting on the ground contemplating my navel.

It is perhaps a rather modern use of the word 'inner', to use it

[1] This is a restatement of the theme of the previous chapter, written for another, and different, audience.

to refer to psychic reality, to claim that there is an inside where personal wealth builds up (or poverty shows) as we make progress in emotional growth and personality establishment.

Here are two places, then, the inside and the outside of the individual. But is this all?

When considering the lives of human beings there are those who like to think superficially in terms of behaviour, and in terms of conditioned reflexes and conditioning; this leads to what is called behaviour therapy. But most of us get tired of restricting ourselves to behaviour or to the observable extrovert life of persons who, whether they like it or not, are motivated from the unconscious. By contrast, there are those who place emphasis on the 'inner' life, who think that the effects of economics and even of starvation itself have but little importance as compared with mystical experience. Infinity for those in the latter category is at the centre of the self, whereas for the behaviourists who think in terms of external reality infinity is reaching out beyond the moon to the stars and to the beginning and the end of time, time that has neither an end nor a beginning.

I am attempting to get in between these two extremes. If we look at our lives we shall probably find that we spend most of our time neither in behaviour nor in contemplation, but somewhere else. I ask: where? And I try to suggest an answer.

An intermediate zone

In psychoanalytic writings and in the vast literature that has been influenced by Freud there can be found a tendency to dwell either on a person's life as it relates to objects or else on the inner life of the individual. In the life of the person who is object-relating it is assumed that there is postulated a state of tension driving towards instinct-satisfaction, or else a basking in the leisure of gratification. A complete statement would include the concept of displacement and all the mechanisms of sublimation. Where excitement has not led to satisfaction the person is caught up in the discomforts that frustration generates, discomforts that include bodily dysfunction and a sense of guilt or the relief that comes from the discovery of a scapegoat or a persecutor.

In regard to mystical experiences, in the literature of psychoanalysis the person we are looking at is asleep dreaming, or if awake is going through a process rather akin to dream-work, but doing this while awake. Every mood is there and the unconscious fantasy of the mood ranges from idealization on the one hand to the awfulness of the destruction of all that is good on the other – bringing the extremes of elation or despair, wellbeing in the body or a sense of being diseased and an urge to suicide.

This is a much simplified and indeed distorted quick review of a vast literature, but I am not attempting to make a comprehensive statement so much as to point out that the written words of psychoanalytic literature do not seem to tell us all that we want to know. What, for instance, are we doing when we are listening to a Beethoven symphony or making a pilgrimage to a picture gallery or reading Troilus and Cressida in bed, or playing tennis? What is a child doing when sitting on the floor playing with toys under the aegis of the mother? What is a group of teenagers doing participating in a pop session?

It is not only: what are we doing? The question also needs to be posed: where are we (if anywhere at all)? We have used the concepts of inner and outer, and we want a third concept. Where are we when we are doing what in fact we do a great deal of our time, namely, enjoying ourselves? Does the concept of sublimation really cover the whole pattern? Can we gain some advantage from an examination of this matter of the possible existence of a place for living that is not properly described by either of the terms 'inner' and 'outer'?

Lionel Trilling (1955) in his Freud Anniversary Lecture says:

'For [Freud] there is an honorific accent in the use of the word [culture], but at the same time, as we cannot fail to hear, there is in what he says about culture an unfailing note of exasperation and resistance. Freud's relation to culture must be described as an ambivalent one.'

I think that in this lecture Trilling is concerned with the same inadequacy that I refer to here, although very different language is being employed.

It will be observed that I am looking at the highly sophisticated adult's enjoyment of living or of beauty or of abstract human contrivance, and at the same time at the creative gesture of a baby who reaches out for the mother's mouth and feels her teeth, and at the same time looks into her eyes, seeing her creatively. For me, playing leads on naturally to cultural experience and indeed forms its foundation.

Now, if my argument has cogency, we have three instead of two human states to compare with each other. When we look at these three sets of the human state we can see that there is one special feature that distinguishes what I am calling cultural experience (or playing) from the other two.

Looking first at external reality and the individual's contact with external reality in terms of object-relating and object-usage, one sees that external reality itself is fixed; moreover, the instinctual endowment that provides the backing for object-relating and object-use is itself fixed for the individual, though it varies according to phase and age, and the individual's freedom to make use of instinctual drives. Here we are more free or less free according to the laws that have been formulated in considerable detail in the psychoanalytic literature.

Let us look next at inner psychic reality, the personal property of each individual in so far as a degree of mature integration has been reached which includes the establishment of a unit self, with the implied existence of an inside and an outside, and a limiting membrane. Here again there is to be seen a fixity that belongs to inheritance, to the personality organization, and to environmental factors introjected and to personal factors projected.

By contrast with these, I suggest that the area available for manœuvre in terms of the third way of living (where there is cultural experience or creative playing) is extremely variable as between individuals. This is because this third area is a product of the *experiences of the individual person* (baby, child, adolescent, adult) in the environment that obtains. There is a kind of variability here that is different in quality from the variabilities that belong to the phenomenon of inner personal psychic reality and to external or shared reality. The extent of this third area can be minimal or maximal, according to the summation of actual experiences.

It is this special kind of variability that concerns me here and now and I wish to examine its meaning. I am making this examination in terms of the position, relative to the individual in the world, in which cultural experience (play) can be said to 'take place'.

A potential space

I put forward for discussion of its value as an idea the thesis that for creative playing and for cultural experience, including its most sophisticated developments, the position is *the potential space* between the baby and the mother. I refer to the hypothetical area that exists (but cannot exist) between the baby and the object (mother or part of mother) during the phase of the repudiation of the object as not-me, that is, at the end of being merged in with the object.

From a state of being merged in with the mother the baby is at a stage of separating out the mother from the self, and the mother is lowering the degree of her adaptation to the baby's needs (both because of her own recovery from a high degree of identification with her baby and because of her perception of the baby's new need, the need for her to be a separate phenomenon).[2]

This is exactly the same as the danger area that is arrived at sooner or later in all psychiatric treatments, the patient having felt secure and viable because of the analyst's reliability, adaptation to need, and willingness to become involved, and now beginning to feel a need to shake free and to achieve autonomy. Like the baby with the mother, the patient cannot become autonomous except in conjunction with the therapist's readiness to let go, and yet any move on the part of the therapist away from a state of being merged in with the patient is under dire suspicion, so that disaster threatens.

It will be remembered that in the example I gave of a boy's use of string (Chapter 1) I referred to two objects as being both *joined and separated* by the string. This is the paradox that I accept and do not attempt to resolve. The baby's separating-out of the world of objects from the self is achieved only through the absence of a space between, the *potential* space being filled in in the way that I am describing.

It could be said that with human beings there can be no separation, only a threat of separation; and the threat is maximally or minimally traumatic according to the experience of the first separatings.

How, one may ask, does separation of subject and object, of baby and mother, seem in fact to happen, and to happen with profit to all concerned, and in the vast majority of cases? And this in spite of the impossibility of separation? (The paradox must be tolerated.)

The answer can be that in the baby's *experience* of life, actually in

---

[2] I have discussed this thesis at length in my paper 'Primary Maternal Preoccupation' (1956).

relation to the mother or mother-figure, there usually develops a degree of confidence in the mother's reliability; or (in another language belonging to psychotherapy) the patient begins to sense that the therapist's concern arises not out of a need for a dependant, but out of a capacity in the therapist to identify with the patient out of a feeling 'if I were in your shoes . . .'. In other words, the mother's or therapist's love does not only mean meeting dependency needs, but it comes to mean affording the opportunity for this baby or this patient to move from dependence to autonomy.

A baby can be fed without love, but loveless or impersonal management cannot succeed in producing a new autonomous human child. Here where there is trust and reliability is a potential space, one that can become an infinite area of separation, which the baby, child, adolescent, adult may creatively fill with playing, which in time becomes the enjoyment of the cultural heritage.

The special feature of this place where play and cultural experience have a position is that it depends for its existence on living experiences, not on inherited tendencies. One baby is given sensitive management here where the mother is separating out from the baby so that the area for play is immense; and the next baby has so poor an experience at this phase of his or her development that there is but little opportunity for development except in terms of introversion or extroversion. The potential space, in the latter case, has no significance, because there was never a built-up sense of trust matched with reliability, and therefore there was no relaxed self-realization.

In the experience of the more fortunate baby (and small child and adolescent and adult) the question of separation in separating does not arise, because in the potential space between the baby and the mother there appears the creative playing that arises naturally out of the relaxed state; it is here that there develops a use of symbols that stand at one and the same time for external world phenomena and for phenomena of the individual person who is being looked at.

The other two areas do not lose significance because of this that I am putting forward as a third area. If we are truly examining human beings, then we must be expected to make observations that can be superimposed, the one on the other. Individuals do relate to the world in ways that involve them in instinctual gratification, either direct or in sublimated forms. Also, we do know the paramount importance of sleep and the deep dreaming that is at the core of the personality, and of contemplation and of relaxed undirected mental inconsequence. Nevertheless, playing and cultural experience are things that we do value in a special way; these link the past, the present, and the future; *they take up time and space*. They demand and get our concentrated deliberate attention, deliberate but without too much of the deliberateness of trying.

The mother adapts to the needs of her baby and of her child who is gradually evolving in personality and character, and this adaptation gives her a measure of reliability. The baby's experience of this reliability over a period of time gives rise in the baby and growing child to a feeling of confidence. The baby's confidence in the mother's reliability, and therefore in that of other people and things, makes possible a separating-out of the not-me from the me. At the same time, however, it can be said that separation is avoided by the filling in of the potential space with creative playing, with the use of symbols, and with all that eventually adds up to a cultural life.

There is in many a failure in confidence which cramps the person's play-capacity because of the limitations of the potential space; likewise there is for many a poverty of play and cultural life because, although the person had a place for erudition, there was a relative failure on the part of those who constitute the child's world of persons to introduce cultural elements at the appropriate phases of the person's personality development.

Naturally, limitations arise out of the relative lack of cultural erudition or even the lack of acquaintance with the cultural heritage which may characterize those actually in charge of a child.

The first need, then, in respect of this that is described in this chapter, is for protection of the baby-mother and baby-parent relationship at the early stage of every boy or girl child's development, so that there may come into being the potential space in which, because of trust, the child may creatively play.

The second need is for those who have care of children of all ages to be ready to put each child into touch with appropriate elements of the cultural heritage, according to the individual child's capacity and emotional age and developmental phase.

It is useful, then, to think of a third area of human living, one neither inside the individual nor outside in the world of shared reality. This intermediate living can be thought of as occupying a potential space, negating the idea of space and separation between the baby and the mother, and all developments derived from this phenomenon. This potential space varies greatly from individual to individual, and its foundation is the baby's trust in the mother *experienced* over a long-enough period at the critical stage of the separation of the not-me from the me, when the establishment of an autonomous self is at the initial stage.

9

MIRROR-ROLE OF MOTHER AND FAMILY IN CHILD DEVELOPMENT[1]

In individual emotional development *the precursor of the mirror is the mother's face*. I wish to refer to the normal aspect of this and also to its psychopathology.

Jacques Lacan's paper 'Le Stade du Miroir' (1949) has certainly influenced me. He refers to the use of the mirror in each individual's ego development. However, Lacan does not think of the mirror in terms of the mother's face in the way that I wish to do here.

I refer only to infants who have sight. The wider application of the idea to cover infants with poor sight or no sight must be left over till the main theme is stated. The bare statement is this: in the early stages of the emotional development of the human

[1] Published in P. Lomas (ed), *The Predicament of the Family: A Psycho-analytical Symposium* (1967). London: Hogarth Press and the Institute of Psycho-Analysis.

infant a vital part is played by the environment which is in fact not yet separated off from the infant by the infant. Gradually the separating-off of the not-me from the me takes place, and the pace varies according to the infant and according to the environment. The major changes take place in the separating-out of the mother as an objectively perceived environmental feature. If no one person is there to be mother the infant's developmental task is infinitely complicated.

Let me simplify the environmental function and briefly state that it involves:

1. Holding
2. Handling
3. Object-presenting.

The infant may respond to these environmental provisions, but the result in the baby is maximal personal maturation. By the word 'maturation' at this stage I intend to include the various meanings of the word 'integration', as well as psychosomatic interrelating and object-relating.

A baby is held, and handled satisfactorily, and with this taken for granted is presented with an object in such a way that the baby's legitimate experience of omnipotence is not violated. The result can be that the baby is able to use the object, and to feel as if this object is a subjective object, and created by the baby.

All this belongs to the beginning, and out of all this come the immense complexities that comprise the emotional and mental development of the infant and child.[2]

Now, at some point the baby takes a look round. Perhaps a baby at the breast does not look at the breast. Looking at the face is more likely to be a feature (Gough, 1962). What does the baby

---

[2] For further and detailed discussion of these ideas the reader can consult my paper 'The Theory of the Parent-Infant Relationship' (1960b).

see there? To get to the answer we must draw on our experience with psychoanalytic patients who reach back to very early phenomena and yet who can verbalize (when they feel they can do so) without insulting the delicacy of what is preverbal, unverbalized, and unverbalizable except perhaps in poetry.

What does the baby see when he or she looks at the mother's face? I am suggesting that, ordinarily, what the baby sees is himself or herself. In other words the mother is looking at the baby and *what she looks like is related to what she sees there*. All this is too easily taken for granted. I am asking that this which is naturally done well by mothers who are caring for their babies shall not be taken for granted. I can make my point by going straight over to the case of the baby whose mother reflects her own mood or, worse still, the rigidity of her own defences. In such a case what does the baby see?

Of course nothing can be said about the single occasions on which a mother could not respond. Many babies, however, do have to have a long experience of not getting back what they are giving. They look and they do not see themselves. There are consequences. First, their own creative capacity begins to atrophy, and in some way or other they look around for other ways of getting something of themselves back from the environment. They may succeed by some other method, and blind infants need to get themselves reflected through other senses than that of sight. Indeed, a mother whose face is fixed may be able to respond in some other way. Most mothers can respond when the baby is in trouble or is aggressive, and especially when the baby is ill. Second, the baby gets settled in to the idea that when he or she looks, what is seen is the mother's face. The mother's face is not then a mirror. So perception takes the place of apperception, perception takes the place of that which might have been the beginning of a significant exchange with the world, a two-way process in which self-enrichment alternates with the discovery of meaning in the world of seen things.

Naturally, there are half-way stages in this scheme of things. Some babies do not quite give up hope and they study the object and do all that is possible to see in the object some meaning that ought to be there if only it could be felt. Some babies, tantalized by this type of relative maternal failure, study the variable maternal visage in an attempt to predict the mother's mood, just exactly as we all study the weather. The baby quickly learns to make a forecast: 'Just now it is safe to forget the mother's mood and to be spontaneous, but any minute the mother's face will become fixed or her mood will dominate, and my own personal need must then be withdrawn otherwise my central self may suffer insult.'

Immediately beyond this in the direction of pathology is predictability, which is precarious, and which strains the baby to the limits of his or her capacity to allow for events. This brings a threat of chaos, and the baby will organize withdrawal, or will not look except to perceive, as a defence. A baby so treated will grow up puzzled about mirrors and what the mirror has to offer. If the mother's face is unresponsive, then a mirror is a thing to be looked at but not to be looked into.

To return to the normal progress of events, when the average girl studies her face in the mirror she is reassuring herself that the mother-image is there and that the mother can see her and that the mother is *en rapport* with her. When girls and boys in their secondary narcissism look in order to see beauty and to fall in love, there is already evidence that doubt has crept in about their mother's continued love and care. So the man who falls in love with beauty is quite different from the man who loves a girl and feels she is beautiful and can see what is beautiful about her.

I will not try to press home my idea, but instead I will give some examples so that the idea I am presenting can be worked over by the reader.

Illustration I

I refer first to a woman of my acquaintance who married and brought up three fine male children. She was also a good support to her husband who had a creative and important job. Behind the scenes this woman was always near to depression. She seriously disturbed her marital life by waking every morning in a state of despair. She could do nothing about it. The resolution of the paralysing depression came each day when at last it was time to get up and, at the end of her ablutions and dressing, she could 'put on her face'. Now she felt rehabilitated and could meet the world and take up her family responsibilities. This exceptionally intelligent and responsible person did eventually react to a misfortune by developing a chronic depressive state which in the end became transformed into a chronic and crippling physical disorder.

Here is a recurring pattern, easily matched in the social or clinical experience of everyone. What is illustrated by this case only exaggerates that which is normal. The exaggeration is of the task of getting the mirror to notice and approve. The woman had to be her own mother. If she had had a daughter she would surely have found great relief, but perhaps a daughter would have suffered because of having too much importance in correcting her mother's uncertainty about her own mother's sight of her.

The reader will already be thinking of Francis Bacon. I refer here not to the Bacon who said: 'A beautiful face is a silent commendation' and 'That is the best part of beauty, which a picture cannot express', but to the exasperating and skilful and challenging artist of our time who goes on and on painting the human face distorted significantly. From the standpoint of this chapter this Francis Bacon of today's date is seeing himself in his mother's face, but with some twist in him or her that maddens both him and us. I know nothing of this artist's private life, and I bring him in only because he forces his way into any present-day discussion of the face and the self. Bacon's faces seem to me to be far removed from perception of the actual; in looking at faces he seems to me to be painfully striving towards being seen, which is at the basis of creative looking.

I see that I am linking apperception with perception by postulating a historical process (in the individual) which depends on being seen:

When I look I am seen, so I exist.

I can now afford to look and see.

I now look creatively and what I apperceive I also perceive.

In fact I take care not to see what is not there to be seen (unless I am tired).

Illustration II

A patient reports: 'I went to a coffee bar last night and I was fascinated to see the various characters there', and she describes some of these characters. Now this patient has a striking appearance, and if she were able to use herself she could be the central figure in any group. I asked: 'Did anyone look at you?' She was able to go over to the idea that she did in fact draw some of the fire, but she had taken along with her a man friend, and she could feel that it was at him that people were looking.

From here the patient and I were together able to make a preliminary survey of the patient's early history and childhood in terms of being seen in a way that would make her feel she existed. Actually the patient had had a deplorable experience in this respect.

This subject then got lost for the time being in other types of material, but in a way this patient's whole analysis revolves round this 'being seen' for what she in fact is, at any one moment; and at times the being actually seen in a subtle way is for her the main thing in her treatment. This patient is particularly sensitive as a judge of painting and indeed of the visual arts, and lack of beauty disintegrates her personality so that she recognizes lack of beauty by herself feeling awful (disintegrated or depersonalized).

Illustration III

I have a research case, a woman who has had a very long analysis. This patient has come through, late in life, to feeling real, and a cynic might say: to what end? But she feels it has been worth while, and I myself have learned a great deal of what I know of early phenomena through her.

This analysis involved a serious and deep regression to infantile dependence. The environmental history was severely disturbing in many respects, but here I am dealing with the effect on her of her mother's depression. This has been worked over repeatedly and as analyst I have had to displace this mother in a big way in order to enable the patient to get started as a person.[3]

Just now, near the end of my work with her, the patient has sent me a portrait of her nurse. I had already had her mother's portrait and I have got to know the rigidity of the mother's defences very intimately. It became obvious that the mother (as the patient said) had chosen a depressed nurse to act for her so that she might avoid losing touch with the children altogether. A lively nurse would automatically have 'stolen' the children from the depressed mother.

This patient has a marked absence of just that which characterizes so many women, an interest in the face. She certainly had no adolescent phase of self-examination in the mirror, and now she looks in the mirror only to remind herself that she 'looks like an old hag' (patient's own words).

---

[3] An aspect of this case was reported by me in my paper 'Metapsychological and Clinical Aspects of Regression within the Psycho-Analytical Set-Up' (1954).

This same week this patient found a picture of my face on a book-cover. She wrote to say she needed a bigger version so that she could see the lines and all the features of this 'ancient landscape'. I sent the picture (she lives away and I see her only occasionally now) and at the same time I gave her an interpretation based on what I am trying to say in this chapter.

This patient thought that she was quite simply acquiring the portrait of this man who had done so much for her (and I have). But what she needed to be told was that my lined face had some features that link for her with the rigidity of the faces of her mother and her nurse.

I feel sure that it was important that I knew this about the face, and that I could interpret the patient's search for a face that could reflect herself, and at the same time see that, because of the lines, my face in the picture reproduced some of her mother's rigidity.

Actually this patient has a thoroughly good face, and she is an exceptionally sympathetic person when she feels like it. She can let herself be concerned with other people's affairs and with their troubles for a limited period of time. How often this characteristic has seduced people into thinking of her as someone to be leaned on! The fact is, however, that the moment my patient feels herself being involved, especially in someone's depression, she automatically withdraws and curls up in bed with a hot water bottle, nursing her soul. Just here she is vulnerable.

Illustration IV
After all this had been written a patient brought material in an analytic hour which might have been based on this that I am writing. This woman is very much concerned with the stage of the establishment of herself as an individual. In the course of this particular hour she brought in a reference to 'Mirror mirror on the wall' etc. and then she said: 'Wouldn't

it be awful if the child looked into the mirror and saw nothing!'

The rest of the material concerned the environment provided by her mother when she was a baby, the picture being of a mother talking to someone else unless actively engaged in a positive relating to the baby. The implication here was that the baby would look at the mother and see her talking to someone else. The patient then went on to describe her great interest in the paintings of Francis Bacon and she wondered whether to lend me a book about the artist. She referred to a detail in the book. Francis Bacon 'says that he likes to have glass over his pictures because then when people look at the picture what they see is not just a picture; they might in fact see themselves.'[4]

After this the patient went on to speak of 'Le Stade du Miroir' because she knows of Lacan's work, but she was not able to make the link that I feel I am able to make between the mirror and the mother's face. It was not my job to give this link to my patient in this session because the patient is essentially at a stage of discovering things for herself, and premature interpretation in such circumstances annihilates the creativity of the patient and is traumatic in the sense of being against the

---

[4] See *Francis Bacon: Catalogue raisonné and documentation* (Alley, 1964). In his Introduction to this book, John Rothenstein writes:

'. . . to look at a painting by Bacon is to look into a mirror, and to see there our own afflictions and our fears of solitude, failure, humiliation, old age, death and of nameless threatened catastrophe.

His avowed preference for having his paintings glazed is also related to his sense of dependence on chance. The preference is due to the fact that glass sets paintings somewhat apart from the environment (just as his daisies and railings set his subjects apart from their pictorial environment), and that glass protects, but what counts more in this case is his belief that the fortuitous play of reflections will enhance his pictures. His dark blue pictures in particular, I heard him observe, gain by enabling the spectator to see his own face in the glass.'

maturational process. This theme continues to be important in this patient's analysis, but it also appears in other guises.

This glimpse of the baby's and child's seeing the self in the mother's face, and afterwards in a mirror, gives a way of looking at analysis and at the psychotherapeutic task. Psychotherapy is not making clever and apt interpretations; by and large it is a long-term giving the patient back what the patient brings. It is a complex derivative of the face that reflects what is there to be seen. I like to think of my work this way, and to think that if I do this well enough the patient will find his or her own self, and will be able to exist and to feel real. Feeling real is more than existing; it is finding a way to exist as oneself, and to relate to objects as oneself, and to have a self into which to retreat for relaxation.

But I would not like to give the impression that I think this task of reflecting what the patient brings is easy. It is not easy, and it is emotionally exhausting. But we get our rewards. Even when our patients do not get cured they are grateful to us for seeing them as they are, and this gives us a satisfaction of a deep kind.

This to which I have referred in terms of the mother's role of giving back to the baby the baby's own self continues to have importance in terms of the child and the family. Naturally, as the child develops and the maturational processes become sophisticated, and identifications multiply, the child becomes less and less dependent on getting back the self from the mother's and the father's face and from the faces of others who are in parental or sibling relationships (Winnicott, 1960a). Nevertheless, when a family is intact and is a going concern over a period of time each child derives benefit from being able to see himself or herself in the attitude of the individual members or in the attitudes of the family as a whole. We can include in all this the actual mirrors that exist in the house and the opportunities the child gets for seeing the parents and others looking at themselves. It should be understood, however, that the actual mirror has significance mainly in its figurative sense.

This could be one way of stating the contribution that a family can make to the personality growth and enrichment of each one of its individual members.

10

INTERRELATING APART FROM INSTINCTUAL DRIVE AND IN TERMS OF CROSS-IDENTIFICATIONS

In this chapter I put into juxtaposition two contrasting statements, each of which in its own way illustrates communication. There are many kinds of inter-communication and a classification of them seems hardly necessary since classification involves the making of artificial boundaries.

The first illustration I wish to give is in the form of a therapeutic consultation with a girl at an early stage of adolescence. This consultation had a result in that it paved the way for a thorough-going analysis which in three years could be counted a success. The point of giving the case, however, is connected not so much with the outcome as with the fact that any case description of this kind illustrates the way in which the psychotherapist acts as a mirror.

I wish to follow up this case description with a theoretical statement illustrating the importance of communication through cross-identifications.

General comment on therapy

Patients who have a restricted capacity for introjective or projective identifying present serious difficulties for the psychotherapist who must needs be subjected to what is called acting out and transference phenomena that have instinctual backing. In such cases the main hope of the therapist is to increase the patient's range in respect of cross-identifications, and this comes not so much through the work of interpretation as through certain specific experiences in the analytic sessions. To arrive at these experiences the therapist must reckon with a time factor, and therapeutic results of an instantaneous kind cannot be expected. Interpretations, however accurate and well-timed, cannot provide the whole answer.

In this particular part of the therapist's work interpretations are more of the nature of verbalization of experiences in the immediate present in the consultation experience, and the concept of an interpretation as a verbalization of the nascent conscious does not exactly apply here.

It must be admitted that there is no clear reason why this material should be included in this particular book, which deals with transitional phenomena. There is, however, a wide range of inquiry that belongs to early functioning before the establishment of the mechanisms in the individual that make sense of classical psychoanalytic theory. The term 'transitional phenomena' could be used to cover all groupings of such early types of functioning and perhaps attention can be usefully drawn to the fact that there are many and various groupings of mental functioning which are of vast importance in research into a psychopathology of the schizoid states. Moreover, it is these same groupings of types of mental functioning that must be studied if a satisfactory account is to be given of the beginning of the individual human personality, and it is undoubtedly true that the cultural aspect of human life including art, philosophy, and religion largely concerns these same phenomena.

INTERVIEW WITH AN ADOLESCENT

A therapeutic consultation[1]

At the time of the consultation Sarah was sixteen years old. She had a brother aged fourteen and a sister aged nine, and the family was intact.

The two parents brought Sarah up from their home in the country and I saw them all three together for three minutes, during which time we renewed contact. I did not refer to the purpose of the visit. The parents then went to the waiting-room. I gave the father my front-door key and said I did not know how long I would be with Sarah.

I purposely omit a considerable quantity of detail accumulated since I first saw Sarah at the age of two years.

Sarah, at sixteen, had straight middle-shade hair down to her shoulders, and she seemed to be healthy physically and a good build for her years. She wore a black plastic coat and looked like an adolescent in a countrified and unsophisticated way. She is intelligent, she has a sense of humour but is basically very serious, and she was quite happy to start our contact with a game.

'What sort of game?'

---

[1] Clinical illustration must necessarily cover much ground that is not immediately relevant, unless the report is severely edited and, by being edited, loses authenticity.

I told her about squiggles, the game with no rules.[2]

(1) My bosh-shot at a squiggle.
(2) My second attempt.

Sarah said she liked school. Mother and father wanted her to come and see me but so did the school. She said: 'I believe I came to see you when I was two, because I didn't like my brother being born; but I can't remember. I think I can just remember something of it.'

She looked at (2) and said: 'Can it be any way up?'

I said: 'There are no rules.' So she made my squiggle into a leaf backwards. I said I liked this, and pointed out its graceful curves.

(3) Hers. She said: 'I'll make it as difficult as possible.' It was a squiggle with a line deliberately added. I used this line as a stick, and made the rest into a schoolmistress teaching by strict methods. She said: 'No, it's not my teacher; she's not a bit like that. It could be a teacher I didn't like at my first school.'
(4) Mine, which she turned into a person. The long hair was meant to be a boy's hair but the face could be of either sex, she said.
(5) Hers, which I tried to turn into a dancer. The original squiggle was better than the result I obtained by drawing.
(6) Mine, which she quickly made into a man resting his nose on a tennis racquet. I said: 'Do you mind playing this game?' and she said: 'No, of course not.'
(7) Hers, a conscious or deliberate drawing, as she herself pointed out. I made it into a kind of bird. She showed what she

[2] There is no need for me to give the actual drawings here; they are referred to by number ((1), (2), etc.) in the text. For similar examples of this technique for communicating see *Therapeutic Consultations in Child Psychiatry* (Winnicott, 1971).

would have done with it (see it upside-down); a sort of man with a top-hat and a big heavy collar.

(8) Mine, which she made into a wonky old music stand. She likes music, and does sing, but she can't play anything.

(9) Here she showed great difficulty in regard to the squiggle technique. She made this drawing and said: 'It's all cramped up, it's not free and spreading.'

> *This was to be the main communication.* Naturally, what was needed was that I should understand it as a communication and be prepared to allow her to expand the idea that it conveyed.
>
> (There is no need for the reader to go right through the further details of this interview, but I give the whole interview because the material is available, and to leave out the remainder would seem like a wasted opportunity to report an adolescent's self-revelation in the context of a professional contact.)

I said: 'It's you, isn't it?'

She said: 'Yes. You see I'm a bit shy.'

I said: 'Naturally, you don't know me and you don't know why you have come or what we are going to do, and . . .'

She carried this on, quite of her own accord, and said: 'You could go on with that – the squiggle is not spontaneous. I'm all the time trying to make an impression because I'm not sure enough of myself. I've been like it for ages. I can't remember being anything else.'

I said: 'It's sad, isn't it?' – as a way of showing that I had heard what she said and that I had feelings because of the implications of what she was telling me.

> Sarah was now in communication with me, and eager to spread herself, revealing herself to herself and to me.

She went on: 'It's stupid, pig-headed. I'm all the time trying to make people like me, respect me, not make a fool of me. It's selfish. It could be helped if I tried. Of course it's all right if I try to amuse people and they laugh. But I sit around all the time wondering what impression I'm making. I still do it, trying to be a roaring success.'

I said: 'But you are not like that here, now.'

She said: 'No, because it doesn't matter. Presumably you are here to find out what's the matter, so you make it possible for me not to have to do all this. You want to find if anything's wrong. I think it's a phase; it's just growing up. I can't help it and I don't know why.'

I asked: 'How do you dream of yourself?'

'Oh, I imagine myself to be calm, collected, casual, a great success, very attractive, slim, with long arms and legs and long hair. I can't draw well (attempting (10)) but I'm striding along, swinging a handbag. I'm not self-conscious or shy.'

'Are you male or female in your dreams?'

'Normally I'm a girl. I don't dream of myself as a boy. I don't want to be one. I have had thoughts of being a boy but not a wish. Of course men have confidence in themselves, and influence, and they get further.'

We looked at the man in (6) and she said: 'He looks hot and it's a sunny day; he's tired and relaxing, squashing his nose against the strings. Or he's depressed.'

I asked about father.

'Daddy doesn't care about himself; he only thinks of his work. Yes, I do love him and admire him very much. My brother has a screen between him and people. He's nice, amiable and sweet. What he thinks is hidden, and he will only talk in a light-hearted way. He's delightful and very funny and intelligent; if he has troubles he keeps them to himself. I'm the opposite. I rush into people's rooms with "Oh I'm so unhappy!" and all that.'

'Can you do that with mother?'

'Oh yes, but at school I can use my friends. Boys more than girls. My very good friend is a girl who is the same as me but older. She always seems to be able to say: "I felt just like that a year ago." Boys don't say things, they don't say I'm stupid. They are kind and they understand better. You see they don't have to *prove* they are manly. My great friend is David. He's rather depressed. He's younger than me. I have lots and lots of friends but only a few real friends who can be counted on to be loyal.'

I asked here about real sleep dreams.

'They are mostly frightening. One I have had several times.'

I asked her to try to illustrate it.

(11) The recurring dream. 'The setting is all quite real and like it is at home. A tall hedge, a rose garden behind, a narrow walk; I am chased by a man; I run. It's all terribly vivid. It's muddy. As I turn the corner I am like running through treacle. I'm not glamorous in all this.'

Later she added: 'He's big and black (not a Negro). He's foreboding. I'm in a panic. No, it's not a sex dream. I don't know what it is.'

(12) 'Another dream that belongs to when I was younger, perhaps six years old. It's our house. I draw it from sideways but that's not as it is in the dream.[3] There's a hedge on the left here that turns into a house. There's a tree behind it. I run in and upstairs and there's a witch in the cupboard. It is like a child's story. The witch has a broomstick and a goose. She walks past me and *looks back*. It is tense in the dream. Everything is buzzing. It's the silence. You expect noise but there's no noise. There is a

---

[3] 'Sideways' may possibly refer to the vantage point for early detection of mother's new pregnancy.

big white goose in the cupboard but it's too big for this tiny cupboard, it really couldn't be in it.

'The way to the hedge (that turned into a house) was downhill, the hill I loved to run down because it's so steep and you hurtle down and lose control. Every step the witch took the step below disappeared, so I couldn't get down or away from her.'

I spoke of this as part of her imagined relationship with her mother.

She said: 'It could be that. But perhaps it could be explained. At that age I was telling lies all the time to mother. (I still tell lies but I try hard to catch myself in time.)'

> She is here referring to a sense of dissociation. Also, there could be a feeling, expressed here, of having been deceived.

I asked if she was pinching things too, and she said: 'No, that has not been a trouble.'

She went on to give examples of her lying at that time, and it was all to do with chores: 'Have you cleaned out your room? Have you polished the floor?' etc. 'I was telling lies all the time, however much mother tried to give me the chance to admit that I was lying. I have lied a lot at school, too, about work. I don't work hard. You see, last term I was happy. But this term I am unhappy. I think I'm growing too quickly; well, not too quickly, just growing. You see I grow rationally and logically much faster than I grow emotionally. Emotionally I've not caught up.'

I asked about menstruation and she said: 'Oh yes, *ages* ago.'

Here Sarah said something that felt important as she said it and it may be that this was the nearest she came to a statement of her position. She said: 'I can't explain; I feel as if I am sitting or standing on top of the spire of a church. There's nothing anywhere round to keep me from falling and I am helpless. I seem to be balancing, just.'

Here I reminded her, although I knew she did not remember it, that she had changed when her mother, who had held her naturally and well, suddenly became unable to hold her when she was one and three-quarters because of being three months pregnant. (There was also the pregnancy when she was six or seven years old.) Sarah seemed to take all this in but she said: 'It's bigger than that. About whatever is chasing me, it's not a man chasing a girl, it's *something* chasing *me*. It's a matter of people *behind* me.'

> At this point the character of the consultation altered and Sarah became a manifestly ill person displaying a psychiatric disorder of paranoid type. By doing this Sarah became dependent on certain qualities that she had found in the professional situation and also she displayed a belief in me of a high degree. She could trust me to deal with her state as an illness or as a distress signal, and not to act in some way that would indicate fear in myself of her illness.

She was now carried away by what she had to say and she went on: 'People may laugh, and unless I catch myself in time and deal with it logically this being laughed at from behind hurts.'

I invited her to try to tell me the worst.

'When I was, say, eleven years old, the beginning of my last school, I liked the junior school [and she described the flowering shrubs at the school and other things she liked there, and the headmistress], but the senior school was snobbish, unkind, and hypocritical.' She said with great feeling: 'I felt *worthless*, and also I was scared physically. I expected to be stabbed, shot, or strangled. Especially stabbed. Like having something pinned on your back, and you didn't know.'

Here, in a different tone of voice, she said: 'Are we getting anywhere?'

> She seemed to need some encouragement if she were to proceed. I of course had no idea what might or might not turn up.

'The worst was (well, it's not so bad now) when I confided in someone something very private, and I had *absolute* faith in them, and *depended* on them not to turn sick on me or to become so that they weren't sympathetic or understanding. But you see, they've changed, they aren't there any more.' She added the comment: 'It's nastiest when I'm crying and I can't find anyone.' And then she withdrew from the position of vulnerability and said: 'Well that's OK, I can deal with that. But it's nastiest when I'm depressed; this makes me uninteresting. I'm gloomy and introspective and all except my girl friend and David go off me.'

> At this point some help was needed from me.

I said: 'The depression means something, something unconscious. [I could use this word with this girl.] You hate the dependable person who has changed and who has ceased to be understanding and dependable, and has perhaps become vindictive. You become depressed instead of feeling hate of the person who was reliable but who changed.'

> This seemed to help.

She went on: 'I dislike people who hurt me' – and then she went straight into a vituperation against a woman at school, allowing herself to leave logic aside and to express her feelings even if they were based on delusion.

> It could be said that she was describing by reliving or re-enacting a maniacal attack she had had at school and about which I did not know. I could now understand why

she had been sent home and recommended to see me. It went like this:

'This woman at school I simply can't stand, I dislike her more than I can possibly say. She's got all the awful things that I feel most easily because I have got them all in myself. It's only herself she thinks of. She's self-centred and vain, and that's me again. And she's cold and hard and nasty. She's a house-mother, looking after the laundry and biscuits and coffee and all that. She doesn't do her job. She sits and entertains all the young male members of the staff, drinking sherry [alcohol isn't allowed in the school] and smoking black Russian cigarettes. And she does all this blatantly in what is really our sitting room.

'So I took a knife. I just threw it and threw it against the door. If I'd thought I'd have known what a noise it was making. And of course in walks this woman. "What! have you lost your senses?" I tried to be polite but she dragged me off saying I must be out of my mind. So I made up a lie of course, and absolutely no one knows it's a lie except my friend and David, and now you. And although she said "I don't believe you", I convinced her.' (She had lied and had said something about trying to mend the handle of the door, and I doubt whether anyone really believed her.)

She had not finished yet, and she was still very excited: 'And there I was wearing a cap of a certain kind [described], and she came and she said, "Take off that ridiculous hat!" I said. "No, why should I?" She said: "Because I told you to. Take it off at once!" So then I screamed and screamed and screamed!'

At this point I remembered that when she changed at one and three-quarter years from being rather a normal child to being an ill one – her mother being three months pregnant and she being quite clearly disturbed by this fact – she had screamed and screamed and screamed. I was in touch with

Sarah's case then, and my notes made fourteen years previously covered the history given me at that time, so that I was sure of my ground.

Sarah went on about the woman: 'You see, inside *she* is as insecure as anyone else. She shouted: "Why don't you scream more?" as if to provoke. So I did, and she said: "Why don't you shout?" So I shouted louder. It was the end of everything. She's old you see.'

I said: 'Forty?'

She said: 'Yes.' And she went on: 'I complained about all the things she does in our room, how we have to knock on her (our) door, and how she complains: "You never come to see me, only to get coffee and biscuits" (which is true).'

This material reveals ambivalence about the alternatives of regressive mechanisms and progressive mechanisms that lead to independence.

A significant part of what went on now has to be unrecorded because I could not take notes.

We discussed all that had happened very seriously. I pointed out that it was a relief to her (Sarah) that she could get to the full expression of her hate, but this was not all the trouble. The fact is that it is not the woman who provokes her that she hates but the good one who is understanding and dependable. It is the woman's reaction in face of provocation that brings out the hate. This is mother being particularly good and changing to being no good, a sudden disillusionment, and this belongs specifically to the moment when mother was six months pregnant when Sarah changed because mother changed.

Sarah kept letting me know that her real mother was all she could wish for in a mother.

I said I knew this but the original sudden disillusionment had set up in her the conviction that if a very good person turns up, then this same person will change, and so be hated; only (I said) I knew Sarah could not reach to this hatred, and to the destruction of the good person. I brought it onto me too, and said: 'There's me here, and you have used me in this special way; but your pattern is to expect me to change and perhaps to betray you.'

At first I thought Sarah did not get the point about the pattern of expectation, but she then showed that she had done so by telling me of her experience with a boy. This boy was marvellous. Sarah could depend on him to any degree. He never let her down and he loved her and he still does. But her despairing self tried to spoil the relationship. She tried not to like him but he went on liking her. After two months of this he said: 'We will not see each other any more, not for a while anyhow. It's too awful.' Sarah was shocked and surprised. So he went away and the relationship broke up. She was quite clear that she had caused it to break up because of her delusion that it would break up from the other end, by a change in him.

I pointed out that this would be the repetition that she dreads but expects because it has become a built-in thing, and that it is based on the fact that mother and father loved and mother became pregnant when she was only one and a half, and at one and three-quarters she could not deal with the change in mother except by developing in herself the conviction that what is very good will always become changed and so will cause her to hate it and to destroy it.

Sarah seemed to get the hang of all this and was now calming down. She then talked of how mother had said this was a phase, and you have to get past living from day to day and develop a philosophy.

She went on to talk about the brilliant David. He is a cynic. 'Cynicism doesn't suit me though,' she said. 'I can't understand it. I trust people naturally. Only I get this depression. David was telling me about existentialism, and this upset me more than I can say. Mother explained how people think they have found the perfect philosophy and then they throw it all away and start all over again. I want to get started. I don't want to seem to be a vegetable. I want to be less selfish, to be more giving and perceptive.'

> Her ideal of herself was so very different from what she found when she examined herself.

I said: 'OK, but I do want you to know that I can see one thing you can't see and that is that your anger is with a good and not with a bad woman. The good woman changes to bad.'

She said: 'That is mother isn't it, but mother is absolutely all right now.'

I said: 'Yes, it's in the pattern in the dream that you can't remember that you destroy your good dependable mother. Your job will be to live through some relationships that do go a bit bad, when you do become a bit angry and a bit disillusioned, and somehow everyone survives.'

We seemed to have finished, but Sarah lingered and then said: 'But how can I stop this bursting into tears?' She told me that really she had been crying for a long time while talking to me but she had been holding back actual tears: 'Else I couldn't talk.'

> Sarah had come through an experience which I had shared. She looked relieved, though we were both tired.

At the end she asked: 'Well, what do I do? I go back to school by train this evening and then what happens? If I don't work I shall be turned out, and I'm bad for David and my friends. But . . .'

So I said: 'Well, clearing all this up is more important than learning history and other lessons, so what about staying home till the end of term? Would mother have you?'

She said this would be a very good idea, and of course she had already thought of it. The school would send her work to do, and in the peace of her home she would be able to mull over all the things we had talked about.

So I arranged this with mother, with Sarah in the room.

Finally, Sarah said to me: 'I think I must have exhausted you.'

> I did get the feeling that Sarah had reached some important feelings, and that she would be able to make use of the next two months at home, with the prospect of a further visit to me in the holidays.

Outcome

This therapeutic consultation had a result that Sarah became eager for a psychoanalytic treatment. Instead of going back to school she started analysis and cooperated fully over the three or four years of the treatment. I am able to report that this treatment ended naturally and can be counted a success.

By the age of twenty-one Sarah was doing well at university and managing her life in a way that showed that she was free of the paranoid intrusions that had compelled her to spoil good relationships.

Tailpiece

I could make a comment on my own behaviour in this one session. Much of the verbalization, as it turned out, was unnecessary, but it must be remembered that at the time I did not know whether this might or might not be the only occasion I would have for giving Sarah help. If I had known that she would go on to have a psychoanalytic treatment I would have said much less except in so far as I needed to let her know that I had heard what she was saying and had noticed what she was feeling and had shown by my reactions that I could contain her anxieties. I would have been more like a human mirror.

INTERRELATING IN TERMS OF CROSS-IDENTIFICATIONS[4]

I shall now discuss inter-communication in terms of the capacity or the absence of a capacity for the use of projective and introjective mental mechanisms.

The gradual development of object-relating is an achievement in terms of the emotional development of the individual. At one extreme object-relating has an instinctual backing and the concept of object-relating here comprises the whole widened range afforded by the use of displacement and symbolism. At the other extreme is the condition that it can be assumed exists at the beginning of the individual's life, in which the object is not yet separated out from the subject. This is a condition to which the word 'merging' is applied when there is a return to it from a state of separation, but it can be assumed that at the beginning there is at least a theoretical stage prior to separation of the not-me from the me (cf. Milner, 1969). The word 'symbiosis' has been brought into play in this area (Mahler, 1969), but for me this is too well rooted in biology to be acceptable. From the observer's point of view there may seem to be object-relating in the primary merged state, but it has to be remembered that at the beginning the object is a 'subjective object'. I have used this term 'subjective object' to allow a discrepancy between what is observed and what is being experienced by the baby (Winnicott, 1962).

In the course of the emotional development of the individual a stage is reached at which the individual can be said to have

---

[4] Published as 'La interrelación en terminos de identificaciones cruzadas' in *Revista de Psicoanalisis*, Tomo 25, No. 3/4 (1968). Buenos Aires.

become a unit. In the language that I have used this is a stage of 'I am' (Winnicott, 1958b) and (whatever we call it) the stage has significance because of the need for the individual to reach *being* before *doing*. 'I am' must precede 'I do', otherwise 'I do' has no meaning for the individual. It is assumed that these developmental stages arrive in tender form at very early stages, but they receive reinforcement from the maternal ego and therefore have a strength in the early stages that belongs to the fact of the mother's adaptation to her baby's needs. Elsewhere I have tried to show that this adaptation to need is not just a matter of the satisfying of instincts but has to be thought of primarily in terms of holding and handling.

Gradually, in healthy development, the developing child becomes autonomous, and becomes able to take responsibility for himself or herself independently of highly adaptive ego support. There is still, of course, vulnerability in the sense that gross environmental failure can result in a loss of the individual's new capacity for maintaining integration in independence.

This stage that I am referring to in terms of 'I am' is very closely allied to Melanie Klein's (1934) concept of the depressive position. At this stage the child can say: 'Here I am. What is inside me is me and what is outside me is not me.' The words 'inside' and 'outside' here refer simultaneously to the psyche and to the soma because I am assuming a satisfactory psycho-somatic partnership, which of course is also a matter of healthy development. There is also the question of the mind, which has to be thought of separately, especially in so far as it becomes a phenomenon split off from the psyche-soma (Winnicott, 1949).

In so far as the individual boy or girl has now reached to a personal organization of inner psychic reality, this inner reality is constantly being matched with samples of external or shared reality. A new capacity for object-relating has now developed, namely, one that is based on an interchange between external reality and samples from the personal psychic reality. This capacity is reflected in the child's use of symbols and in creative playing and, as I have tried to show, in the gradual ability of the child to use cultural potential in so far as it is available in the immediate social environment (see Chapter 7).

Now let us examine the very important new development that belongs to this stage, namely, the establishment of interrelationships based on introjection and projection mechanisms. This is more closely allied to affection than it is to instinct. Although the ideas that I am referring to stem from Freud, nevertheless our attention was drawn to them by Melanie Klein who usefully distinguished between projective and introjective identification, and emphasized the importance of these mechanisms (Klein, 1932, 1957).

Case: a woman aged forty years, unmarried

I wish to give a detail from an analysis in order to illustrate in a practical way the importance of these mechanisms. It is not necessary to say more about this woman patient than to refer to the impoverishment of her life because of her inability to 'stand in other persons' shoes'. She was either isolated or else made tentative efforts at object-relating with instinctual backing. There were very complex reasons for this patient's specific difficulty but it could be said that she lived in a world that was all the time distorted for her by her own inability to feel concerned with what the other person was feeling. Along with this there was her inability to feel that others knew what she was like or what she was feeling.

It will be understood that in the case of a patient like this, who was able to do a job and only occasionally was so depressed that she was suicidal, this condition was an organized defence and not entirely an original incapacity persisting from infancy. As often happens in psychoanalysis, one has to study mechanisms in terms of their use in a highly sophisticated defence organization in order to get an idea about the primary condition. In my patient there were areas in which she had very acute empathy and sympathy as, for instance, in regard to all downtrodden persons in the world. These of course included all groups that are treated by other groups in a degraded way, and also women. She assumed from very deep down in her nature that women were degraded and third class. (Along with this men represented her split-off male element, so that she could not let men come into her life in a practical way. This theme of the split-off other-sex elements is significant, but since it is not the main theme of the chapter it will be left aside here; it is developed elsewhere, see Chapter 5.)

There had been some signs in the weeks before the time of the session that I am reporting that the patient was beginning to recognize her lack of capacity for projective identification. She averred on several occasions, and did so rather aggressively as if expecting to be contradicted, that there was no point in feeling sorry for anyone that was dead. 'You can feel sorry for those who are left behind if they were fond of the dead person, but the dead person is dead, and that is the end of the matter.' This was logical and there was nothing beyond the logic for my patient. The cumulative effect of this kind of attitude made my patient's friends sensible of something lacking, however intangible, in her personality, so that the range of my patient's friendships was limited.

In the course of the session I am describing the patient reported the death of a man for whom she had great respect. She saw that she was referring to the possible death of the analyst, myself, and her loss of the special part of me that she still had need of. One could almost feel that she knew that there was something callous about her need for her analyst to live simply and solely on account of the residue of her need for him (cf. Blake, 1968).

There was a period here in which my patient said that she wanted to cry infinitely and for no clear reason, and I pointed out to her that in saying this she was also saying that it was not possible for her to cry. She responded with the words: 'I can't cry here because this is all I get and I can't waste the time' – and then she broke down with the words: 'Everything is nonsense!' and sobbed.

There was an end of a phase here, and the patient now started telling me dreams she had written down.

A male pupil at the school where she teaches may decide to leave and get a job. She pointed out that here again was cause for grief; it was like losing a child. Here was one area where projective identification had come to be a very important mechanism during the last year or two of the analysis. The children she was teaching, especially if talented, represented herself, so that their achievements were hers, and if they left the school it was a disaster. Unsympathetic treatment of these pupils who represented herself, especially those who were boys, made her feel herself insulted.

Here then was an area recently developed in which projective identification had become possible, and although clinically one could see that it was pathologically compulsive this did not prevent it from being a valuable thing in terms of what children need from a teacher. The important thing was that these pupils were not third-class citizens for her, although they seemed to have that position in terms of her picture of the school in which many of the staff seemed to act as if they despised the children.

In a long analysis this was the first time that I was able to use material to point out the fact of projective identification. I did not, of course, use the technical term. This boy who had turned up in the dream and who might leave and take a job instead of going on to fulfilment in the school could be accepted by my patient (his teacher) as the place where she was finding something of herself. What she was finding there was in fact a split-off male element (but, as I have already mentioned, this important detail belongs to a different presentation of the case-material).

The patient was now able to discuss cross-identifications and to look back on certain experiences of the recent past in which she had acted in a way that was incredibly callous if one did not know of her lack of capacity for projective or introjective identifying. She had in fact planted herself as an ill person on an ill person, and had claimed full attention 'completely regardless' (as she said, looking at herself in a new way) of the other person's reality situation.[5] At this point she usefully introduced the word 'alienation' in description of the feeling that she has always had because of there being no cross-identifications, and she was able to go further and to say that a great deal of her jealousy of the friend (who represented a sibling) on whom she had planted her ill self had to do with the friend's positive capacity for living and communicating in terms of cross-identifications.

My patient then went on to describe an experience of invigilating at an examination where one of her boy pupils was being examined in art. He painted a wonderful picture and then he painted it all out. She found this terrible to watch, and she knows that some of her colleagues interfere at such a point, which of course is not fair in terms of examination ethics. It was a severe blow to her narcissism watching the good picture being withdrawn, and not being able to rescue it. So strong was her use of the boy as an expression of her own living experience that it was with the greatest difficulty that she brought herself to see that in terms of this boy the withdrawal of the good

---

[5] In another language that belongs to the analysis of psychoneurosis this was an unconscious sadistic action, but this language is useless here.

picture could have value because, perhaps, he could not summon the courage to do so well and to be praised, or because he decided that in order to get through the examination he must comply with the expectations of the examiners and this would involve a betrayal of his true self. Perhaps he must fail.

We can see here a mechanism that might have resulted in her being herself a bad examiner, but that was being reflected in her finding the conflicts in the children who represented part of herself, especially her male or executive element. On this particular occasion that I am reporting my patient was able to see with scarcely any help at all from the analyst that these children were not living for her benefit, although she had felt that they were doing exactly that. She had the idea that at times she could say that she came alive only in terms of the children into whom she had projected parts of herself.

We can understand from the way in which this mechanism was working in this patient how it is that in some of the Kleinian expositions on this subject the language used implies that the patient is actually forcing stuff into someone else, or into an animal, or into the analyst. This is particularly apposite when the patient is in a depressed mood, but not experiencing this mood because of having pushed the material of the depressive fantasy into the analyst.

The next dream was of a small child being slowly poisoned by a chemist. This had to do with the reliance that the patient still has on drug therapy, although drug-dependence is not the main feature of her case. She does need help in getting to sleep and so, as she said, although she hates the drugs, and does all she can to avoid them, it is worse if she does not sleep and has to manage to live in the day in a state of sleep-deprivation.

The material that followed continued with this theme which had appeared in a new way in this particular session of this long analysis. Among the subsequent associations the patient quoted from a poem by Gerard Manley Hopkins:

I am soft sift
In an hourglass – at the wall
Fast, but mined with a motion, a drift,
And it crowds and it combs to the fall;
I steady as a water in a well, to a poise, to pane,
But roped with, always, all the way down from the tall
Fells or flanks of the voel, a vein . . .

The idea implied was that she was completely at the mercy of some power like gravity, drifting, with no control over anything. Often she feels this about the analysis and the analyst's decisions in regard to times and lengths of session. We could see here the idea of a life without cross-identifications, and this means that the analyst (or God or fate) can supply nothing by way of projective identification, that is to say, with an understanding of the needs of the patient.

From here my patient went on to other vitally important matters which do not concern this specific subject of cross-identifications but which have to do with the implacable nature of the struggle between her woman self and her split-off male element.

She described herself as being in gaol, locked up, completely out of control of things, identified with the sand in the hourglass. It became clear that she had evolved a technique for projective identifications of the split-off male element, giving her some vicarious experience in terms of pupils and other people into whom she could project this part of herself; as compared with this, however, there was a striking absence of a capacity for projective identification in respect of her woman self. This patient has no difficulty in thinking of herself all the time as a woman but she knows and always has known that a woman is a 'third-class citizen' and she has also always known that nothing can be done about this.

She was now able to feel her dilemma in terms of the divorce or separation between her woman self and the split-off male element, and emerging out of this came a new view of her father and mother, one that gave them a warm and devoted inter-relationship as married persons and as parents. In an extreme moment of recovery of good memories the patient felt once more her face up against her mother's scarf, this carrying with it the idea of a state of being merged in with mother and linking, at any rate theoretically, with the primary state before the separation of object from subject or before the establishment of the object as objectively perceived and truly separate or external.

> There were now several memories bolstering up what there had developed during the session, memories of a good environment in which she, the patient, was an ill person. Always this patient has exploited and needed to exploit the unfortunate environmental factors that have had aetiological significance. The patient had often reported the relief she got on a certain occasion when she saw her parents giving each other a kiss when she was a little girl. She now felt the meaning of this in a new and deeper way and believed in the genuineness of the feelings that underlay the act.

In this session there could be seen the process of the develop-ment of a capacity for projective identification, this new capacity bringing with it a new type of relationship of a kind that this patient had not been able to achieve in her life. Along with this came a new realization of what the relative absence of this has meant in terms of the impoverishment of her relationship to the world and of the world to her, especially in respect of inter-communication. It should be added that along with this new capacity for *empathy* there had arrived in the transference a new ruthlessness and a capacity to make big demands on the analyst, the assumption being that the analyst, now an external or separate phenomenon, *would look after himself*. She felt that the analyst would be glad that the patient had become able to achieve greed, which is in an important sense equivalent to love. The analyst's function is survival.

There was a change in this patient. Within two weeks she had even come to say that she felt sorry for her mother (who was dead) because she was unable to go on wearing the jewellery that she had handed on to my patient, but that my patient could not wear. My patient was scarcely aware that, only recently, she had claimed that one could not feel sorry for someone who was dead, which was true in cold logic. Now she was *imaginatively* living, or wanting to live through wearing the jewellery, in order to give her dead mother some life, even if only a little, and vicariously.

The relation of changes to the therapeutic process

The question arises, how do these changes in the capacity of the patient take place? Certainly the answer is *not* that they come about through the operation of interpretation directly bearing on the working of the mental mechanism. I say this in spite of the fact that in the clinical material I have given I did make one verbal reference of a direct kind; in my opinion the work had already been done when I allowed myself this luxury.

There was a long history of psychoanalysis in this case, several years done with a colleague, and three years done with myself.

It would be fair to suggest that the capacity of the analyst to use projective mechanisms, perhaps the most important passport to psychoanalytic work, gradually becomes introjected. But this is not all, nor is it fundamental.

In this case, and in similar cases, I have found that the patient has needed phases of regression to dependence in the transference, these giving experience of the full effect of adaptation to need that is in fact based on the analyst's (mother's) ability to identify with the patient (her baby). In the course of this kind of *experience* there is a sufficient quantity of being merged in with the analyst (mother) to enable the patient to live and to relate without the need for projective and introjective identificatory mechanisms. Then comes the painful process whereby the object is separated out from the subject, and the analyst becomes separated off and is placed outside the omnipotent control of the patient. The analyst's survival of the destructiveness that belongs to and follows this change enables a new thing to happen, which is the patient's *use* of the analyst, and the initiation of a new relationship based on cross-identifications (see Chapter 6). The patient can now begin to stand imaginatively in the analyst's shoes, and (at the same time) it is possible and good for the analyst to stand in the patient's shoes from a position, that is, of having his own feet on the ground.

The favourable result, then, is of the nature of an evolution in the transference, taking place because of the continuation of the analytic process.

Psychoanalysis has drawn a full measure of attention to the operation of instinct, and to sublimation of instinct. It is important to remember that there are significant mechanisms for object-relating that are not drive-determined. I have emphasized the elements in playing that are not drive-determined. I have given examples to illustrate interrelating that belongs to exploitation of the dependence and adaptation phenomena that have a natural place in babyhood and parenthood. I have also pointed out that much of our lives is spent interrelating in terms of cross-identifications.

Now I wish to refer to the relationships that specifically belong to the area of parental management of adolescent rebellion.

11

CONTEMPORARY CONCEPTS OF ADOLESCENT DEVELOPMENT AND THEIR IMPLICATIONS FOR HIGHER EDUCATION[1]

PRELIMINARY OBSERVATIONS

My approach to this vast subject must derive from the area of my especial experience. The remarks that I may make must be cast in the mould of the psychotherapeutic attitude. As a psychotherapist I naturally find myself thinking in terms of

the emotional development of the individual;

the role of the mother and of the parents;

---

[1] Part of a symposium given at the 21st Annual Meeting of the British Student Health Association at Newcastle upon Tyne, 18 July 1968.

the family as a natural development in terms of childhood needs;

the role of schools and other groupings seen as extensions of the family idea, and relief from set family patterns;

the special role of the family in its relation to the needs of adolescents;

the immaturity of the adolescent;

the gradual attainment of maturity in the life of the adolescent;

the individual's attainment of an identification with social groupings and with society, without too great a loss of personal spontaneity;

the structure of society, the word being used as a collective noun, society being composed of individual units, whether mature or immature;

the abstractions of politics and economics and philosophy and culture seen as the culmination of natural growing processes;

the world as a superimposition of a thousand million individual patterns, the one upon the other.

The dynamic is the growth process, this being inherited by each individual. Taken for granted, here, is the good-enough facilitating environment, which at the start of each individual's growth and development is a *sine qua non*. There are genes which determine patterns and an inherited tendency to grow and to achieve maturity, and yet nothing takes place in emotional growth except in relation to the environmental provision, which must be good enough. It will be noticed that the word 'perfect' does not enter into this statement – perfection belongs to machines, and the imperfections that are characteristic of human adaptation to need are an essential quality in the environment that facilitates.

Basic to all this is the idea of *individual dependence*, dependence being at first near-absolute and changing gradually and in an ordered way to relative dependence and towards independence. Independence does not become absolute, and the individual seen as an autonomous unit is in fact never independent of environment, though there are ways by which in maturity the individual may *feel* free and independent, as much as makes for happiness and for a sense of having a personal identity. By means of cross-identifications the sharp line between the me and the not-me is blurred.

All I have done so far is to enumerate various sections of an encyclopaedia of human society in terms of a perpetual ebullition on the surface of the cauldron of individual growth seen collectively and recognized as dynamic. The bit that I can deal with here is necessarily limited in size, and it is important therefore for me to place what I shall say against the vast back-screen of humanity, humanity that can be viewed in many different ways and that can be looked at with the eye at the one or the other end of the telescope.

Illness or health?

As soon as I leave generalities and start to become specific I must choose to include this and to reject that. For instance, there is the matter of personal psychiatric illness. Society includes all its individual members. The structure of society is built up and maintained by its members who are psychiatrically healthy. Nevertheless it must needs contain those who are ill – for instance, society contains:

> the immature (immature in age);
>
> the psychopathic (end-product of deprivation – persons who, *when hopeful*, must make society acknowledge the fact of their deprivation, whether of a good or loved object or of a

satisfactory *structure* that could be relied on to stand the strains that arise out of spontaneous movement);

the neurotic (bedevilled by unconscious motivation and ambivalence);

the moody (hovering between suicide and some alternative, which may include the highest achievements in terms of contribution);

the schizoid (who have a life-work already set out for them, namely the establishment of themselves, each one as an individual with a sense of identity and of feeling real);

the schizophrenic (who cannot, at least in ill phases, feel real, who may (at best) achieve something on a basis of living by proxy).

To these we must add the most awkward category – one that includes many persons who get themselves into positions of authority or responsibility – namely: the paranoid, those who are dominated by a system of thought. This system must be constantly shown to explain everything, the alternative (for the individual ill that way) being acute confusion of ideas, a sense of chaos, and a loss of all predictability.

In any description of psychiatric illness there is overlapping. People do not group themselves nicely into illness groupings. It is this that makes psychiatry so difficult for physicians and surgeons to understand. They say: 'You have the disease and we have (or will have in a year or two) the cure.' No psychiatric label exactly meets the case, and least of all the label 'normal' or 'healthy'.

We could look at society in terms of illness, and how its ill members one way and another compel attention, and how society becomes coloured by the illness groupings that start in the individuals; or indeed we could examine the way in which families and social units may produce individuals who are psychiatrically healthy except that the social unit that happens to be theirs at any one time distorts them or renders them ineffectual.

I have not chosen to look at society in this way. I have chosen to look at society in terms of its healthiness, that is, in its growth or perpetual rejuvenation naturally out of the health of its psychiatrically healthy members. I say this even though I do know that at times the proportion of psychiatrically unhealthy members in a group may be too high, so that the healthy elements even in their aggregate of health cannot carry them. Then the social unit becomes itself a psychiatric casualty.

I therefore intend to look at society as if it were composed of psychiatrically healthy persons. Even so, society will be found to have problems enough! Enough indeed!

It will be noted that I have not used the word 'normal'. This word is too well tied up with facile thinking. But I do believe that there is such a thing as psychiatric health, and this means that I feel justified in studying society (as others have done) in terms of its being the statement in collective terms of individual growth towards personal fulfilment. The axiom is that since there is no society except as a structure brought about and maintained and constantly reconstructed by individuals, there is no personal fulfilment without society, and no society apart from the collective growth processes of the individuals that compose it. And we must learn to cease looking for the world-citizen, and be contented to find here and there persons whose social unit extends beyond the local version of society, or beyond nationalism, or beyond the boundaries of a religious sect. In effect we need to accept the fact that psychiatrically healthy persons depend for their health and for their personal fulfilment on loyalty to a delimited area of society, perhaps the local bowls club. And why not? It is only if we look for Gilbert Murray everywhere that we come to grief.

The main thesis

A positive statement of my thesis brings me immediately to the tremendous changes that have taken place in the last fifty years in regard to the importance of good-enough mothering. This includes fathers, but fathers must allow me to use the term 'maternal' to describe the total attitude to babies and their care. The term 'paternal' must necessarily come a little later than maternal. Gradually the father as male becomes a significant factor. And then follows the family, the basis of which is the union of fathers and mothers, in a sharing of responsibility for this that they have done together, that which we call a new human being – a baby.

Let me refer to the maternal provision. We now know that it does matter how a baby is held and handled, that it matters who it is that is caring for the baby, and whether this is in fact the mother, or someone else. In our theory of child care, continuity of care has become a central feature of the concept of the facilitating environment, and we see that by this continuity of environmental provision, and only by this, the new baby in dependence may have a continuity in the line of his or her life, not a pattern of reacting to the unpredictable and for ever starting again (cf. Milner, 1934).

I can refer here to Bowlby's (1969) work: the two-year-old child's reaction to loss of mother's person (even temporary), if beyond the time-stretch of the baby's capacity to keep alive her image, has found general acceptance though it has yet to be fully exploited; but the idea behind this extends to the whole subject of continuity of care and dates from the beginning of the baby's personal life, that is, before the baby objectively perceives the whole mother as the person she is.

Another new feature: as child psychiatrists we are not just concerned with health. I wish this were true of psychiatry in general. We are concerned with the richness of the happiness that builds up in health and *does not build up* in psychiatric ill health, even when the genes could take the child towards fulfilment.

We now look at slums and poverty not only with horror, but also with an eye open to the possibility that for a baby or a small child a slum family may be more secure and 'good' as a facilitating environment than a family in a lovely house where there is an absence of the common persecutions.[2] Also, we can feel it is worthwhile to consider the essential differences that exist between social groups in terms of accepted customs. Take swaddling, as opposed to the infant's permission to explore and to kick that obtains almost universally in society as we know it in Britain. What is the local attitude to pacifiers, to thumb-sucking, to auto-erotic exercises in general? How do people react to the natural incontinences of early life and their relation to continence? And so on. The phase of Truby King is still in process of being lived down by adults trying to give their babies the right to discover a personal morality, and we can see this in a reaction to indoctrination that goes to the extreme of extreme permissiveness. It might turn out that the difference between the white citizen of the United States and the black-skinned citizen of that country is not so much a matter of skin colour as of breast-feeding. Incalculable is the envy of the white bottle-fed population of the black people who are mostly, I believe, breast-fed.

It may be noticed that I am concerned with unconscious motivation, something that is not altogether a popular concept. The data I need are not to be culled from a form-filling questionnaire. A computer cannot be programmed to give motives that are unconscious in the individuals who are the guinea pigs of an investigation. This is where those who have spent their lives doing psychoanalysis must scream out for sanity against the

[2] Overcrowding, starvation, infestation, the constant threat from physical disease and disaster and from the laws promulgated by a benevolent society.

insane belief in surface phenomena that characterizes computer-ized investigations of human beings.

More confusion

Another source of confusion is the glib assumption that if mothers and fathers bring up their babies and children well there will be less trouble. Far from it! This is very germane to my main theme, because I wish to imply that when we look at adolescence, where the successes and failures of baby and child care come home to roost, some of the present-day troubles belong to the positive elements in modern upbringing and in modern attitudes to the rights of the individual.

If you do all you can to promote personal growth in your offspring, you will need to be able to deal with startling results. If your children find themselves at all they will not be contented to find anything but the whole of themselves, and that will include the aggression and destructive elements in themselves as well as the elements that can be labelled loving. There will be this long tussle which you will need to survive.

With some of your children you will be lucky if your minis-trations quickly enable them to use symbols, to play, to dream, to be creative in satisfying ways, but even so the road to this point may be rocky. And in any case you will make mistakes and these mistakes will be seen and felt to be disastrous, and your children will try to make you feel responsible for setbacks even when you are not in fact responsible. Your children simply say: I never asked to be born.

Your rewards come in the richness that may gradually appear in the personal potential of this or that boy or girl. And if you succeed you must be prepared to be jealous of your children who are getting better opportunities for personal development than you had yourselves. You will feel rewarded if one day your daughter asks you to do some baby-sitting for her, indicating thereby that she thinks you may be able to do this satisfactorily; or if your son wants to be like you in some way, or falls in love with a girl you would have liked yourself, had you been younger. Rewards come indirectly. And of course you know you will not be thanked.

DEATH AND MURDER IN THE ADOLESCENT PROCESS[3]

I now jump to the re-enactment of these matters as they affect the task of parents when their children are at puberty, or in the throes of adolescence.

Although a great deal is being published concerning the individual and social problems that appear in this decade, wherever adolescents are free to express themselves, there may be room for a further personal comment on the content of adolescent fantasy.

In the time of adolescent growth boys and girls awkwardly and erratically emerge out of childhood and away from dependence, and grope towards adult status. Growth is not just a matter of inherited tendency, it is also a matter of a highly complex interweaving with the facilitating environment. If the family is still there to be used it is used in a big way; and if the family is no longer there to be used, or to be set aside (negative use), then small social units need to be provided to contain the adolescent growth process. The same problems loom at puberty that were present in the early stages when these same children were relatively harmless toddlers or infants. It is worth noting that, if you have done well at the early stages and are still doing well, you cannot count on a smooth running of the machine. In fact

[3] Published under the title 'Adolescent Process and the Need for Personal Confrontation' in *Pediatrics*, Vol. 44, No. 5, Part 1 (1969).

you can expect troubles. Certain troubles are inherent at these later stages.

It is valuable to compare adolescent ideas with those of childhood. If, in the fantasy of early growth, there is contained *death*, then at adolescence there is contained *murder*. Even when growth at the period of puberty goes ahead without major crises, one may need to deal with acute problems of management because growing up means taking the parent's place. *It really does*. In the unconscious fantasy, growing up is inherently an aggressive act. And the child is now no longer child-size.

It is legitimate, I believe, as well as useful, to look at the game 'I'm the King of the castle'. This game belongs to the male element in boys and girls. (The theme could also be stated in terms of the female element in girls and boys, but I cannot do this here.) This is a game of early latency, and at puberty it becomes changed into a life-situation.

'I'm the King of the castle' is a statement of personal being. It is an achievement of individual emotional growth. It is a position that implies the death of all rivals or the establishment of dominance. The expected attack is shown in the next words: 'And you're the dirty rascal' (or 'Get down you dirty rascal'). Name your rival and you know where you are. Soon the dirty rascal knocks the King over and in turn becomes King. The Opies (1951) refer to this rhyme. They say that the game is exceedingly old, and that Horace (20 B.C.) gives the children's words as:

> Rex erit qui recte faciet;
> Qui non faciet, non erit.

We need not think that human nature has altered. What we need to do is to look for the everlasting in the ephemeral. We need to translate this childhood game into the language of the unconscious motivation of adolescence and society. If the child is to become adult, then this move is achieved over the dead body of an adult. (I must take it for granted that the reader knows that I am referring to unconscious fantasy, the material that underlies playing.) I know, of course, that boys and girls may manage to go through this stage of growth in a continued setting of accord with actual parents, and without necessarily manifesting rebellion at home. But it is wise to remember that rebellion belongs to the freedom you have given your child by bringing him or her up in such a way that he or she exists in his or her own right. In some instances it could be said: 'You sowed a baby and you reaped a bomb.' In fact, this is always true, but it does not always look like it.

In the total unconscious fantasy belonging to growth at puberty and in adolescence, there is *the death of someone*. A great deal can be managed in play and by displacements, and on the basis of cross-identifications; but, in the psychotherapy of the individual adolescent (and I speak as a psychotherapist), there is to be found death and personal triumph as something inherent in the process of maturation and in the acquisition of adult status. This makes it difficult enough for parents and guardians. Be sure it makes it difficult also for the individual adolescents themselves who come with shyness to the murder and the triumph that belong to maturation at this crucial stage. The unconscious theme may become manifest as the experience of a suicidal impulse, or as actual suicide. Parents can help only a little; the best they can do is to *survive*, to survive intact, and without changing colour, without relinquishment of any important principle. This is not to say they may not themselves grow.

A proportion at adolescence will become casualties or will attain to a kind of maturity in terms of sex and marriage, perhaps becoming parents like the parents themselves. This may do. But somewhere in the background is a life-and-death struggle. The situation lacks its full richness if there is a too easy and successful avoidance of the clash of arms.

This brings me to my main point, the difficult one of the immaturity of the adolescent. Mature adults must know about this and must believe in their own maturity as never before or after.

It will be appreciated that it is difficult to state this without being misunderstood, since it so easily sounds like a down-grading to talk of immaturity. But this is not intended.

A child of any age (say six years) may suddenly need to become responsible, perhaps because of the death of a parent or because of the break-up of a family. Such a child must be pre-maturely old and must lose spontaneity and play and carefree creative impulse. More frequently, an adolescent may be in this position, suddenly finding himself or herself with the vote or with the responsibility for running a college. Of course, if circumstances alter (if, for instance, you become ill or die, or you are in financial straits) then you cannot avoid inviting the boy or girl to become a responsible agent before the time is ripe; perhaps younger children have to be cared for or educated, and there may be an absolute need for money to live. However, it is different when, as a matter of deliberate policy, the adults hand over responsibility; indeed, to do this can be a kind of letting your children down at a critical moment. In terms of the game, or the life-game, you abdicate just as they come to killing you. Is anyone happy? Certainly not the adolescent, who now becomes the establishment. Lost is all the imaginative activity and striving of immaturity. Rebellion no longer makes sense, and the adolescent who wins too early is caught in his own trap, must turn dictator, and must stand up waiting to be killed – to be killed not by a new generation of his own children, but by siblings. Naturally, he seeks to control them.

Here is one of the many places where society ignores unconscious motivation at its peril. Surely the everyday material of the psychotherapist's work could be used a little by sociologists and by politicians, as well as by ordinary people who are adults – that is to say, adult in their own limited spheres of influence, even if not always in their private lives.

What I am stating (dogmatically in order to be brief) is that the adolescent is immature. Immaturity is an essential element of health at adolescence. There is only one cure for immaturity and that is the *passage of time* and the growth into maturity that time may bring.

Immaturity is a precious part of the adolescent scene. In this is contained the most exciting features of creative thought, new and fresh feeling, ideas for new living. Society needs to be shaken by the aspirations of those who are not responsible. If the adults abdicate, the adolescent becomes prematurely, and by false process, adult. Advice to society could be: for the sake of adolescents, and of their immaturity, do not allow them to step up and attain a false maturity by handing over to them responsibility that is not yet theirs, even though they may fight for it.

With the proviso that the adult does not abdicate, we may surely think of the strivings of adolescents to find themselves and to determine their own destiny as the most exciting thing that we can see in life around us. The adolescent's idea of an ideal society is exciting and stimulating, but the point about adolescence is its immaturity and the fact of not being responsible. This, its most sacred element, lasts only a few years, and it is a property that must be lost to each individual as maturity is reached.

I constantly remind myself that it is the state of adolescence that society perpetually carries, not the adolescent boy or girl who, alas, in a few years becomes an adult, and becomes only too soon identified with some kind of frame in which new babies, new children, and new adolescents may be free to have vision and dreams and new plans for the world.

Triumph belongs to this attainment of maturity by growth process. Triumph does not belong to the false maturity based on a facile impersonation of an adult. Terrible facts are locked up in this statement.

Nature of immaturity

It is necessary to look for a moment into the nature of immaturity. We must not expect the adolescent to be aware of his or her immaturity, or to know what the features of immaturity are. Nor do we need to understand at all. What counts is that the adolescents' challenge be met. Met by whom?

I confess that I feel I am insulting this subject by talking about it. The more easily we verbalize, the less are we effectual. Imagine someone talking down to adolescents and saying to them: 'The exciting part of you is your immaturity!' This would be a gross example of failure to meet the adolescent challenge. Perhaps this phrase 'a meeting of the challenge' represents a return to sanity, because understanding has become replaced by confrontation. The word 'confrontation' is used here to mean that a grown-up person stands up and claims the right to have a personal point of view, one that may have the backing of other grown-up people.

Potential at adolescence

Let us look and see what sorts of things adolescents have not reached.

The changes of puberty take place at varying ages, even in healthy children. Boys and girls can do nothing but wait for these changes. This waiting around puts a considerable strain on all, but especially on the late developers; so, the late ones can be found imitating those who have developed early, and this leads to false maturities based on identifications rather than on the innate growth process. In any case, the sexual change is not the only one. There is a change towards physical growth and the acquisition of real strength; therefore, real danger arrives which gives violence a new meaning. Along with strength come cunning and know-how.

Only with the passage of time and the experience of living can a boy or girl gradually accept responsibility for all that is happening in the world of personal fantasy. Meanwhile there is a strong liability for aggression to become manifest in suicidal form; alternatively, aggression turns up in the form of a search for persecution, which is an attempt to get out of the madness of a presecutory delusional system. Where persecution is delusionally expected, there is a liability for it to be provoked in an attempt to get away from madness and delusion. One psychiatrically ill boy (or girl) with a well-formed delusional system can spark off a group system of thought and lead to episodes based on provoked persecution. Logic holds no sway once the delicious simplification of a persecutory position has been achieved.

But most difficult of all is the strain felt in the individual belonging to the unconscious fantasy of sex and the rivalry that is associated with sexual object-choice.

The adolescent, or the boy and girl who are still in process of growing, cannot yet take responsibility for the cruelty and the suffering, for the killing and the being killed, that the world scene offers. This saves the individual at this stage from the extreme reaction against personal latent aggression, namely suicide (a pathological acceptance of responsibility for all the evil that is, or that can be thought of). It seems that the latent sense of guilt of the adolescent is terrific, and it takes years for the development in an individual of a capacity to discover in the self the balance of the good and the bad, the hate and the destruction that go with love, within the self. In this sense, maturity belongs to later life, and the adolescent cannot be expected to see beyond the next stage, which belongs to the early twenties.

It is sometimes taken for granted that boys and girls who 'hop in and out of bed', as the saying goes, and who achieve intercourse (and perhaps a pregnancy or two), have reached sexual maturity. But they themselves know that this is not true, and they begin to despise sex as such. It's too easy. Sexual maturity needs to include all the unconscious fantasy of sex, and the individual needs ultimately to be able to reach to an acceptance of all that turns up in the mind along with object-choice, object-constancy, sexual satisfaction, and sexual interweaving. Also, there is the sense of guilt that is appropriate in terms of the total unconscious fantasy.

Construction, reparation, restitution

The adolescent cannot yet know what satisfaction there can be attained from participation in a project that needs to include within itself the quality of dependability. It is not possible for the adolescent to know how much the job, because of its social contribution, lessens the personal sense of guilt (that belongs to unconscious aggressive drives, closely linked with object-relating and with love) and so helps to lessen the fear within, and the degree of suicidal impulse or accident proneness.

Idealism

One of the exciting things about adolescent boys and girls can be said to be their idealism. They have not yet settled down into disillusionment, and the corollary of this is that they are free to formulate ideal plans. Art students, for instance, can see that art could be taught well, so they clamour for art to be taught well. Why not? What they do not take into account is the fact that there are only a few people who can teach art well. Or students see that physical conditions are cramped and could be improved, so they scream. It is for others to find the money. 'Well,' they say, 'just abandon the defence programme and spend the cash on new university buildings!' It is not for the adolescent to take a long-term view, which may come more naturally to those who have lived through many decades and begin to grow old.

All of this is absurdly condensed. It omits the prime significance of friendship. It omits a statement of the position of those who make a life without marriage or with marriage postponed. And it leaves out the vital problem of bisexuality, which becomes resolved but never entirely resolved in terms of heterosexual object-choice and of object-constancy. Also, a great deal has been taken for granted that has to do with the theory of creative playing. Moreover, there is the cultural heritage; it cannot be expected that, at the age of adolescence, the average boy or girl has more than an inkling of man's cultural heritage, for one must work hard at this even to know about it. At sixty years old these who are boys and girls now will be breathlessly making up for lost time in the pursuit of the riches that belong to civilization and its accumulated by-products.

The main thing is that adolescence is more than physical puberty, though largely based on it. Adolescence implies growth, and this growth takes time. And, while growing is in progress, *responsibility must be taken by parent-figures*. If parent-figures abdicate, then the adolescents must make a jump to a false maturity and lose their greatest asset: freedom to have ideas and to act on impulse.

Summary

In brief, it is exciting that adolescence has become vocal and active, but the adolescent striving that makes itself felt over the whole world today needs to be met, needs to be given reality by an act of confrontation. Confrontation must be personal. Adults are needed if adolescents are to have life and liveliness. Confrontation belongs to containment that is non-retaliatory, without vindictiveness, but having its own strength. It is salutary to remember that the present student unrest and its manifest expression may be in part a product of the attitude we are proud to have attained towards baby care, and child care. Let the young alter society and teach grown-ups how to see the world afresh; but, where there is the challenge of the growing boy or girl, there let an adult meet the challenge. And it will not necessarily be nice.

In the unconscious fantasy these are matters of life and death.

TAILPIECE

I am proposing that there is a stage in the development of human beings that comes before objectivity and perceptibility. At the theoretical beginning a baby can be said to live in a subjective or conceptual world. The change from the primary state to one in which objective perception is possible is not only a matter of inherent or inherited growth process; it needs in addition an environmental minimum. It belongs to the whole vast theme of the individual travelling from dependence towards independence.

This conception-perception gap provides rich material for study. I postulate an essential paradox, one that we must accept and that is not for resolution. This paradox, which is central to the concept, needs to be allowed and allowed for over a period of time in the care of each baby.

REFERENCES

ALLEY, RONALD (1964). *Francis Bacon: Catalogue Raisonné and Documenta-tion*. London: Thames & Hudson.

AXLINE, VIRGINIA MAE (1947). *Play Therapy: The Inner Dynamics of Child-hood*. Boston, Mass.: Houghton Mifflin.

BALINT, MICHAEL (1968). *The Basic Fault: Therapeutic Aspects of Regression*. London: Tavistock Publications.

BETTELHEIM, BRUNO (1960). *The Informed Heart: Autonomy in a Mass Age*. New York: Free Press; London: Thames & Hudson, 1961.

BLAKE, YVONNE (1968). Psychotherapy with the more Disturbed Patient. *Brit. J. Med. Psychol.*, **41**.

BOWLBY, JOHN (1969). *Attachment and Loss*. Volume 1, *Attachment*. London: Hogarth Press and the Institute of Psychoanalysis; New York: Basic Books.

DONNE, JOHN (1962). *Complete Poetry and Selected Prose*. Edited by J. Hayward. London: Nonesuch Press.

ERIKSON, ERIK (1956). The Problem of Ego Identity. *J. Amer. Psychoanal. Assn.*, **4**.

FAIRBAIRN, W. R. D. (1941). A Revised Psychopathology of the Psychoses and Psychoneuroses. *Int. J. Psycho-Anal.*, **22**.

'FIELD, JOANNA' (M. MILNER) (1934). *A Life of One's Own*. London: Chatto & Windus. Harmondsworth: Penguin Books, 1952.

FOUCAULT, MICHEL (1966). *Les Mots et les choses*. Paris: Éditions Gallimard. Published in English under the title *The Order of Things*. London: Tavistock Publications; New York: Pantheon, 1970.

FREUD, ANNA (1965). *Normality and Pathology in Childhood*. London: Hogarth Press and the Institute of Psycho-Analysis.

FREUD, SIGMUND (1900). *The Interpretation of Dreams*. Standard Edition, Vols. 4 and 5.

—— (1923). *The Ego and the Id*. Standard Edition, Vol. 19.

—— (1939). *Moses and Monotheism*. Standard Edition, Vol. 23.

GILLESPIE, W. H. (1960). *The Edge of Objectivity: An Essay in the History of Scientific Ideas*. Princeton, N.J.: Princeton University Press.

GOUGH, D. (1962). The Behaviour of Infants in the First Year of Life. *Proc. Roy. Soc. Med.*, **55**.

GREENACRE, PHYLLIS (1960). Considerations regarding the Parent-Infant Relationship. *Int. J. Psycho-Anal.*, **41**.

HARTMANN, HEINZ (1939). *Ego Psychology and the Problem of Adaptation*. New York: International Universities Press; London: Imago, 1958.

HOFFER, WILLI (1949). Mouth, Hand, and Ego-Integration. *Psychoanal. Study Child*, **3/4**.

—— (1950). Development of the Body Ego. *Psychoanal. Study Child*, **5**.

KHAN, M. MASUD R. (1964). The Function of Intimacy and Acting Out in Perversions. In R. Slovenko (ed.), *Sexual Behavior and the Law*. Springfield, Ill.: Thomas.

—— (1969). On the Clinical Provision of Frustrations, Recognitions and Failures in the Analytic Situation. *Int. J. Psycho-Anal.*, **50**.

KLEIN, MELANIE (1932). *The Psycho-Analysis of Children*. Rev. edn. London: Hogarth Press and the Institute of Psycho-Analysis, 1949.

—— (1934). A Contribution to the Psychogenesis of Manic-Depressive States. In *Contributions to Psycho-Analysis 1921–1945*. London: Hogarth Press and the Institute of Psycho-Analysis, 1948.

—— (1940). Mourning and its relation to Manic-Depressive States. In *Contributions to Psycho-Analysis 1921–1945*.

—— (1957). *Envy and Gratitude*. London: Tavistock Publications.

KNIGHTS, L. C. (1946). *Explorations*. London: Chatto & Windus. Harmondsworth: Penguin Books (Peregrine series), 1964.

KRIS, ERNST (1951). Some Comments and Observations on Early Autoerotic Activities. *Psychoanal. Study Child*, **6**.

LACAN, JACQUES (1949). Le Stade du Miroir comme formateur de la fonction du je, telle qu'elle nous est révélée dans l'expérience psychanalytique. In *Écrits*. Paris: Éditions du Seuil, 1966.

LOMAS, P. (ed.) (1967). *The Predicament of the Family*. London: Hogarth Press and the Institute of Psycho-Analysis.

LOWENFELD, MARGARET (1935). *Play in Childhood*. Bath: Cedric Chivers, 1969.

MAHLER, MARGARET S. (1969). *On Human Symbiosis and the Vicissitudes of Individuation*. Vol. 1, *Infantile Psychosis.*. London: Hogarth Press and the Institute of Psycho-Analysis.

MIDDLEMORE, MERRELL P. (1941). *The Nursing Couple*. London: Hamish Hamilton Medical Books.

MILLER, ARTHUR (1963). *Jane's Blanket*. New York and London: Collier/ Macmillan.

MILNE, A. A. (1926). *Winnie the Pooh*. London: Methuen.

MILNER, M. (1934). *A Life of One's Own*. See under 'Field, Joanna'.

—— (1952). Aspects of Symbolism in Comprehension of the Not-Self. *Int. J. Psycho-Anal.*, **33**.

—— (1957). *On Not Being Able to Paint*. Revised edn. London: Heinemann.

—— (1969). *The Hands of the Living God*. London: Hogarth Press and the Institute of Psycho-Analysis.

OPIE, IONA and PETER (eds.) (1951). *The Oxford Dictionary of Nursery Rhymes*. Oxford: Clarendon Press.

PLAUT, FRED (1966). Reflections about Not Being Able to Imagine. *J. Anal. Psychol.*, **11**.

RIVIERE, JOAN (1936). On the Genesis of Psychical Conflict in Earliest Infancy. *Int. J. Psycho-Anal.*, **17**.

SCHULZ, CHARLES M. (1959). *Peanuts Revisited – Favorites, Old and New*. New York: Holt, Rinehart & Winston.

SHAKESPEARE, WILLIAM. *Hamlet, Prince of Denmark*.

SOLOMON, JOSEPH C. (1962). Fixed Idea as an Internalized Transitional Object. *Amer. J. Psychotherapy*, **16**.

SPITZ, RENÉ (1962). Autoerotism Re-examined: The Role of Early Sexual Behaviour Patterns in Personality Formation. *Psychoanal. Study Child*, **17**.

STEVENSON, O. (1954). The First Treasured Possession: A Study of the Part Played by specially Loved Objects and Toys in the Lives of Certain Children. *Psychoanal. Study Child*, **9**.

TRILLING, LIONEL (1955). Freud: Within and Beyond Culture. In *Beyond Culture*. Harmondsworth: Penguin Books (Peregrine series), 1967.

WINNICOTT, D. W. (1931). *Clinical Notes on Disorders of Childhood*. London: Heinemann.

WINNICOTT, D. W. (1935). The Manic Defence. In *Collected Papers: Through Paediatrics to Psycho-Analysis*. London: Tavistock Publications, 1958.

—— (1941). The Observation of Infants in a Set Situation. Ibid.

—— (1945). Primitive Emotional Development. Ibid.

—— (1948). Paediatrics and Psychiatry. Ibid.

—— (1949). Mind and its Relation to the Psyche-Soma. Ibid.

—— (1951). Transitional Objects and Transitional Phenomena. Ibid.

—— (1952). Psychoses and Child Care. Ibid.

—— (1954). Metapsychological and Clinical Aspects of Regression within the Psycho-Analytical Set-up. Ibid.

—— (1956). Primary Maternal Preoccupation. Ibid.

—— (1958a). *Collected Papers: Through Paediatrics to Psycho-Analysis*. London: Tavistock Publications.

—— (1958b). The Capacity to be Alone. In *The Maturational Processes and the Facilitating Environment*. London: Hogarth Press and the Institute of Psycho-Analysis, 1965.

—— (1959–64). Classification: Is there a Psychoanalytic Contribution to Psychiatric Classification? Ibid.

—— (1960a). Ego Distortion in Terms of True and False Self. Ibid.

—— (1960b). The Theory of the Parent-Infant Relationship. Ibid.

—— (1962). Ego Integration in Child Development. Ibid.

—— (1963a). Communicating and Not Communicating leading to a Study of Certain Opposites. Ibid.

—— (1963b). Morals and Education. Ibid.

—— (1965). *The Maturational Processes and the Facilitating Environment*. London: Hogarth Press and The Institute of Psycho-Analysis.

—— (1966). Comment on Obsessional Neurosis and 'Frankie'. *Int. J. Psycho-Anal.*, **47**.

—— (1967a). The Location of Cultural Experience. *Int. J. Psycho-Anal.*, **48**.

—— (1967b). Mirror-role of Mother and Family in Child Development. In P. Lomas (ed.), *The Predicament of the Family: A Psycho-analytical Symposium*. London: Hogarth Press and the Institute of Psycho-Analysis.

—— (1968a). Playing: Its Theoretical Status in the Clinical Situation. *Int. J. Psycho-Anal.*, **49**.

—— (1968b). La Schizophrénie infantile en termes d'échec d'adaptation. In *Recherches*, (Special issue: 'Enfance aliénée', II), December. Paris.

—— (1971). *Therapeutic Consultations in Child Psychiatry*. London: Hogarth Press and the Institute of Psycho-Analysis.

WULFF, M. (1946). Fetishism and Object Choice in Early Childhood. *Psychoanal. Quart.*, **15**.

INDEX

acting out: psychotherapy 161

adaptation: good-enough mothers 13–14, 16, 144–8, 176

adolescent development 186–203; cross-identifications 162–75

affection: interrelationships 177

aggression: adolescent development 193, 195, 200; creativity 94–5; destruction of object 124–5

amnesia 29–30

anal erotic organization 12

annihilation 125

anxiety: playing 70; search for the self 74–5; separation from the mother 131–2; transitional objects 10; transitional phenomena 5–6

apperception: mirror-role of mother 151, 154

art: creativity 91–3; search for the self 73

auto-erotism 1; first possessions 6, 19; playing 52–4; thumb-sucking 4–5; transitional objects 2–3

autonomy: adolescent development 188; development of 176; potential space 145–6

Axline, Virginia Mae 68

babbling: thumb-sucking 5

Bacon, Francis 153–4, 157

Balint, Michael 74

beauty: mirror-role of mother 152, 154–5

behaviour therapy 141

being: development of 176; female element 108–9, 110, 111–12, 114

being alone 64

being seen: mirror-role of mother 154–5

benign regression 74

bisexuality 96–114

body: playing 69–70

borderline cases 116–17, 134–5

Bowlby, John 191

breast: destruction of 124; illusion 15–18; male and female elements 107, 109–10, 111–12; object-relating and object-usage 119; transitional objects 12

cathexis 118, 136

climax: playing 70

comforters 9
communication: cross-identifications 160–85; playing 73, 74–6
compliance 87–8
concentration: playing 69
contemplation 147
contiguity: cultural experience 136, 139
continuity: cultural experience 136, 139
creativity: dreaming 42; interpretations 116; mirror-role of mother 151; origins 87–114; play 136–7; search for the self 71–87
cross-identifications 160–85
cultural experience 128–39; adolescent development 202; location 140–8
culture: definition 133–4

daydreaming 35–50
death: adolescent development 194–203
death instinct 95
delusions: adolescent development 200; attacks on analyst 123–4; creativity 88–90
denial: separation 20–7
dependence 20; adolescent development 188; environment 95; potential space 145–8
depression: fantasy 28; mirror-role of mother 153
depressive position 176
destruction: creativity 94–5; of object 120–7
disillusionment 13–19
dissociation: creativity 90; fantasying 35–50; male and female elements 101–14

doing: development of 176; fantasying 35–50; male element 108–9, 110, 111, 114
dreaming 35–50, 147
drive: male and female elements 108–9, 111
drug addiction 27

education: adolescent development 186–203
ego: cultural experience 135–6
ego-relatedness: cultural experience 136
empathy 177–84
enjoyment: location of 142–3
environment: adolescent development 187–8, 194; creativity 91–2, 95–6; cultural experience 135, 144; destruction of creativity 91–2; development 89; good-enough mothering 191; male and female elements 104, 110; mirror-role of mother 150–1; object-usage 118, 120; playing 72
Erikson, Erik 64, 109–10
erotogenic zones 107
excitement: object-relating 118; playing 69–70
experience 3; cultural 133–9, 140–8, 202; illusory 4; object-relating 132–3
external life 3
external objects: first possession 19; transitional objects 13
external reality: creativity 87–91; cultural experience 142–4; object-relating 176–7; place where we live 140; playing 55–6, 69, 71–2

faces: mirror-role of mother 149–59

faeces: creativity 73
Fairbairn, W. R. D. 136
fantasy 35–50; adolescent
    development 194–203;
    aggressive and destructive 94–5;
    destruction of object 121, 125–6;
    masturbation 53; transitional
    phenomena 27–34
fathers 191, 193–4
fear: playing 67
female element 97–114;
    interrelationships 183
fetishism: transitional objects 12
first possessions 2–8, 19
formlessness 45–50, 80; playing 86;
    search for the self 74
free association 74–5
Freud, Anna 54
Freud, Sigmund: creativity 94–5;
    cultural experience 128–9;
    culture 143; living 141–2
frustration: good-enough mothers
    14; weaning 17

gender 96–114; interrelationships
    182–3
good-enough mothers: adaptation
    13–14, 16, 144–8, 176; adolescent
    development 191–4; female
    element 109–10; illusion-
    disillusionment 15–18; object-
    relating and object-usage 119
gratification 141–2
guilt: adolescent development
    200–1; creativity 94

hallucinations: creativity 88–90
Hamlet 112–13
handling 150, 176, 191
happiness 191–2
health 188–90; creativity 94–5

higher education: adolescent
    development 186–203
history: myths 133–4
history-taking 10–11
holding 150, 176, 191
homosexuality 25; dissociation of
    female element 105–6
human nature 3–4

idealism: adolescent development
    201–2
identifications 115–27
identity: fantasying 46; male and
    female elements 107–10, 114;
    play 64
illness 188–90
illusion 4, 13–19
imagination: fantasying 36–7, 42–3
immaturity: adolescent
    development 197–203
impotence 105
imprinting 107
indebtedness 3
infinity 141
inner reality 3–4; cultural
    experience 143–4; enjoyment
    142–3; object-relating 176–7;
    place where we live 140–1;
    playing 55–6, 69, 71–2
instinct: male and female
    elements 108–9, 111; object-
    relating 132–3
instinct-satisfaction 141–2
instinctual arousal: playing 70
instinctual gratification 147
interchange 15
internal objects: first possession
    19; transitional objects 12–13
internal representation 20
interpretation 116, 123–4; cross-
    identifications 161; playing 68,

76, 82–6; psychoanalysis 116, 123–4, 184
interrelating 160–85
introjection: cross-identifications 175; interrelationships 177–85; psychotherapy 161

Klein, Melanie 12–13; creativity 94–5; depressive position 176; interrelationships 177; playing 53–4
Knights, L. C. 113
Kris, Ernst 53

Lacan, Jacques 149, 157
language: transitional objects 6
living: cultural experience 133–5; destruction of creativity 91–3, 95–6; fantasying 35–50; place where we live 140–8; playing 67–8

madness: separation from the mother 131–2
magical control: breast 15; play 63–4
male element 97–114; adolescent development 195; interrelationships 183
malignant regression 74
masturbation: playing 52–4
Mead, Margaret 109–10
men: male and female elements 97–114
mental representations 129; transitional object as symbol of the mother 131–2
merging 175
Miller, Arthur 55
Milne, A. A. 54–5
Milner, Marion 52, 132

mirror-role of mother 149–60
moodiness 189
mother-fixation: transitional objects 9
mothers: adaptation 13–14, 16, 144–8, 176; adolescent development 191–4; cultural experience 135–7, 144–8; death of 29–30; depression of 155–6; female element 109–12; good-enough 13–14, 15–18, 109–10, 119, 144–8, 176, 191–4; illusion-disillusionment 15–18; mirror-role 149–60; object-relating and object-usage 119; playing 63–7, 69; potential space 55–63, 144–8; separation from 20–7, 28–34, 131–2; transitional object as symbol of 130–2
murder: adolescent development 194–203
mystical experience: place where we live 140–2
myths 133–4

narcissism 20; mirror-role of mother 152
neurosis 189
non-purposive state: search for the self 74
non rapid eye movements (NREM) 75
nostalgia: separation 30–1
not-me objects 2–8; mirror-role of mother 150
NREM see non rapid eye movements

objectivity: creativity 88–90; fantasy 27–34; play 63
object-presenting 150

object-relating 115–27; cross-identifications 175; cultural experience 143; dissociation of female element 106, 107–14; experience of 132–3; fantasying 38; inner reality 176–7; living 141–2

objects: cultural experience 135; destruction of 120–7; thumb-sucking 5; transitional objects 2–3

object-seeking 136

object-usage 115–27; cultural experience 143; transitional object as symbol of the mother 130–2

omnipotence: destruction of object 120–3; dissociation of male or female elements 104; fantasying 37–8; illusion 15; object-use 150; play 63–4

Opie, Iona and Peter 195

oral erotism 1; thumb-sucking 4–5; transitional objects 2–3

oral satisfaction: first possessions 2

oral tradition 133–4

original sin: death instinct 95

paradox: transitional objects and phenomena 119

paranoia 189

parents see fathers; mothers

penis envy 98, 100–1

perception: mirror-role of mother 151–4

perversion: transitional phenomena 25–6

place: playing 55–63, 71–2

Plaut, Fred 137–8

playground 64

playing: location of 71–2, 129–38; search for the self 71–87;

theoretical statement 51–70; time and place 55–63

pleasure: play 136

poetry: fantasying 48

potential space: cultural experience 135–9, 144–8; playing 55–63, 64, 69, 72

preoccupation: playing 69

primary dissociation 35–50

projection: cross-identifications 175; interrelationships 177–85; object-relating 118; psychotherapy 161

psychoanalysis: attacks on analyst 122–4; borderline cases 116–17; creativity 93; cultural experience 138; interpretation 116, 123–4, 184; mirror-role of mother 158; mystical experiences 142; playing 56, 72

psychoneurosis 117; cultural experience 134–5

psychopathy 188–9

psychosis: borderline cases 116–17; cultural experience 138; living 134–5

psychosomatic disorder 117

psychotherapy: cross-identifications 160, 161–2; mirror-role of mother 158; playing 51–2, 56, 67–8, 72, 76

rapid eye movements (REM) 75

reality principle: aggression 125; object-usage 119–22

reality-testing 3–4; illusion 15; transitional objects 12

rebellion: adolescent development 194–203

regression: depression of mother 155–6

relaxation: search for the self 74–5
REM *see* rapid eye movements
resistance: interpretation 68
responsibility: adolescent
    development 197–202
reverberation 75–6

satisfaction: playing 70
schizoid patients 189; creativity
    88–90; living 134–5
schizophrenia 89–90, 117, 189
Schulz, Charles M. 54–5
search for the self 71–87
self: male and female elements
    107–8, 111–12; mirror-role of
    mother 149–59; search for the
    71–87
separation: cross-identifications
    175; fantasying 28–34;
    mirror-role of mother 150;
    potential space 145–8;
    transitional object as symbol of
    the mother 131–2; transitional
    phenomena 20–7
setting: search for the self 74
sexuality: adolescent development
    200–1; bisexuality 96–114
Shakespeare, William 112–13
society: illness 188–90
soothers 10, 11
Spitz, René 53
stammering 56–8
stealing 114
string 20–7, 57–8
subjective object 95; cross-
    identifications 175; cultural
    experience 135; male and female
    elements 107–9
subjectivity: creativity 88–90;
    fantasy 27–34
subjects: destruction of object

120–7; object-relating 118–19;
    object-usage 119–20
sublimation 128–9, 142–3
suffering: destruction of creativity
    91–2
suicide 37; adolescent development
    196, 200; destruction of
    creativity 92
symbiosis 175
symbolism: dreaming 48; potential
    space 146–7; separation 30–4;
    transitional objects 8, 130–2
sympathy 177–84

talisman 54
thumb-sucking 4–5; fantasying 36,
    40; first possession 19; weaning
    10, 11
time: playing 55–63
tradition 133–4
transference 116, 124, 161
transitional objects 1–34; female
    element 109–10; as symbol of
    the mother 130–2
transitional phenomena 1–34;
    dependence 95; playing 54–5,
    71–2; psychotherapy 161–2
trauma: separation from the
    mother 131–2
Trilling, Lionel 142–3
trust: cultural experience 138, 139;
    playing 69; potential space
    146–7; search for the self 74–6

weaning: illusion-disillusionment
    17–18; transitional objects 9–10
women: creativity 97;
    interrelationships 182–3; male
    and female elements 97–114
words: transitional objects 6
Wulff, M. 54